Practical Parenting

For Single Moms

Lois M. Breit

Copyright © 2020 by Lois M. Breit

ISBN: 978-0-9887398-5-7

Editing by Loren Latourelle & Emily Harris Greene

Cover by Vicki Higgins/Higgins Design

All Scriptures listed in the footnotes can be found in the Holy Bible, or at www. biblegateway.com. Select the translation desired.

All scripture references are from the New International Version (NIV) unless otherwise noted. NLT is the New Living Translation; MSG is The Message translation.

Printed in the United States of America.

Dedicated to all single moms
and to my children, who taught me as much as
I taught them.

Special thanks to
Doug, Peter, Jill, Benjamin, and Pamela for your forgiving
hearts, enduring love, and continued patience.

Also special thanks to Heather King for her help in the
development of this book, and Pamela Beaudry for her
knowledge and input on foster care and social work.

Additional books by Lois Breit
*30 Days of Choices** (Devotional Book)
*30 Days of Hope** (Devotional Book)
*8 Weeks of Love** (Bible study)
Single Mom Ministry—A Church Leadership Guidebook
All of these books may be ordered from Amazon.com.
Available in English and Spanish

www.loisbreit.com — www.singlemamas.org

Stories shared in this book are true, but names have been changed.

INTRODUCTION

"My help comes from the Lord, the maker of heaven and earth."
—Psalm 121:2

Whether married or single, parenting is a hard job! It requires all the knowledge you can gain from books, websites, local parenting resources, and other parents who have completed this journey well.

The topics I cover in this book are primarily directed to help moms parenting alone. However, these practical parenting tips are useful for all parents. (This includes military moms, married moms, grandparents raising their grandchildren, foster moms, and even single dads.) We *all* need help in parenting our children!

Parenting always includes times of laughter and moments of tears, some wins, and some losses. You will try your hardest and still make mistakes. You will face many messy moments— maybe even messy years. However, the key component of parenting must always be an unconditional, forgiving, teachable, restorative love; and the hope of creating a better family legacy.

No matter your parenting status or the ages of your children, I hope this book will help you along your journey.

NOTE

Parents, you can do everything right, and your child can still choose to do everything wrong. We cannot control our children. We can only teach, guide, and encourage to the best of our ability. Our children will decide which path they will take in life. I believe if we do our part and pray hard, we leave room for God to do His part. Never give up on learning new techniques, trying new things, or believing in yourself and your kids.

DISCLAIMER

I have never been a perfect mom. I still don't do everything right—even with my now-grown children. But I believe when children are taught and experience love and forgiveness, it leaves little room for anger or resentment to grow.

FAITH

Because faith played such a profound part in my family's journey, it will be expressed throughout this book. But whether you're a person of faith or not, this book will offer many practical tips as you navigate your world of parenting.

Don't try to be perfect but try to *perfect* parenting
methods that work for *your* family.

CONTENTS

Chapter 1

Parenting Begins with You

*No discipline is enjoyable while it is happening—it's painful!
But afterward there will be a peaceful harvest of right living
for those who are trained in this way.* —Hebrews 12:11 (NLT)

Whether you have one child or five, you need all the help you
can get to bring order, security, and hope to your family—and it
begins with you!

This chapter is about learning self-discipline so you'll be better
equipped to train your children for a more peaceful home and
successful life. This scripture speaks truth; establishing a new
discipline is not enjoyable at the time, but a reward will follow.

The dictionary describes discipline as "control gained by
enforcing obedience or order; orderly or prescribed conduct or
pattern of behavior; self-control."[1]

Simply put, discipline is about *training* your will to become a
benefit, not a detriment, to you and your family.

Before you endeavor to establish some new self-discipline and
parenting skills, gather a strong cheerleading section of friends,
family, and believers to encourage you along the way. Also, look

---

1 Merriam Webster Dictionary, "discipline"

at this chapter and the suggestions in this book through the eyes of your family. Tackle the things that matter most to you. Don't try to change all your old habits at once! Be kind to yourself. Take one step at a time.

Because you teach by example (how you *actually* respond to life), you must learn to discipline yourself before you can successfully discipline your children. Therefore, the first step in training your children is to discipline (train) yourself. So, let's spend a few moments assessing your own current level of self-discipline before we tackle the discipline (training) of your children.

Ask yourself these simple questions—honestly and without feeling guilty:

1. Do you get up, get to work, and get your kids to school on time?

2. What is your morning attitude? Is it positive, negative, or indifferent/zombie like?

3. Do you feel or act like a victim?

4. Are you frequently angry or impatient?

5. Do you take on too much self-guilt or guilt for your child?

6. Do you find yourself blaming others, rather than taking responsibility for *your* actions?

7. Have you given your young children adult roles?

   Responsibilities beyond their age or ability?

   Involving them in adult/parent concerns or decisions they're not emotionally mature enough to understand or that might cause them to be anxious or fearful?

   Has your child unwittingly become your emotional partner? Do they feel they need to comfort you or try to make *you* happy?

8. Are you willing to change your own negative behaviors before expecting your children to change theirs?

I emphasize again: do not take on guilt over current or past habits as you answer these questions. This book is to help you recognize areas of concern, make new choices, and develop parenting skills that will benefit your individual family.

I know developing new habits is not easy, especially during crisis and exhaustion. But as you gradually regain control over your emotions, disciplines, and life choices, you'll begin to see a difference in your family.

I had to make many changes to my attitude and outlook when I became a single mom. It was a process as I moved past grief and self-pity. I wanted my life to be different, but the longer I waited for my life circumstance to change, the longer we lived in chaos. Making new choices, setting new goals, and thinking differently about myself was the start of a new journey that changed our family dynamic and our future.

Change is a process. It will take time, but you can do this!

If you're ready to make some changes, where do you begin?

Eliminate excuses, delays, and further self-pity.

Get counseling if needed. Ask your pastor, doctor, or social worker for counseling references for your depression, out-of-control anger, or other emotional issues you seem unable to control consistently.

Don't expect others to take on your parenting role or responsibilities. *Accepting* help and *expecting* help are two different things.

Look for joy in your life. Don't just focus on the burdens surrounding you.

Believe you have value and that God loves you, regardless of your past.

If you're having a hard day, avoid giving in to it. Call a positive friend for encouragement. Ask your children to share a funny story from school or buy a joke book to share with your kids. Be creative and *look* for joy.

Attitudes Matter

Attitudes are contagious. Your words have power and often dictate your actions. If negative thoughts dominate, begin to change your self-talk vocabulary. Try using some of these phrases to begin your positive self-talk disciplines:

"I can" to replace "I can't".

"I'll try" to replace "I'll fail".

"I will" instead of "I won't".

These few words can start you on a new positive self-talk discipline that changes your mind set—making the seemingly impossible things in your life become possible. These new thoughts will help you move away from your past in both words and actions.

Keep Your Promises

I know you want your children to trust you and have confidence in your promises to them. So, if you tell your child you'll be doing something, or going somewhere, be sure to follow through with your plans. If you back out at the last minute, it's not only a great disappointment to your child (and any others involved in the plan), but it also erodes trust.

Be a Reliable Employee

This will help you keep your job, get promotions, and garner references for future jobs. It also sets an example for your children to follow, and that they too can count on you.

Develop Calm Reactions

When children know you'll react calmly to daily crises, they'll be more open to sharing their problems or mistakes with you. Trust is built when your home is stable, and your children know what to expect.

This takes a lot of practice for those with a short fuse. (I'm one of them). Be kind to yourself but keep working on patient reactions.

Here are a few examples to help you stay calm:

- Don't speak or respond immediately. Take a breath and think about the outcome you want to see happen before responding.

- Separate yourself from the situation. Send your child to their room to cool down. Let your child know you'll respond shortly.

- Take time to think about what the appropriate reaction should be: a punishment, lost privilege, length of time, etc.

- What is the teachable moment in this situation? How can you turn a bad choice into a positive learning opportunity for their future?

- Avoid words like "you/I never" or "you/I always."

- Do not bring up their past mistakes and add them to the current situation.

- Choose a friend who will keep you accountable for your attitudes, actions, and choices.

- Avoid sarcasm. It's a subtle form of anger and a way to avoid confronting the underlying issue.

If you really want to change a habit, find someone you respect and trust to partner with you. A person who has shown maturity in the area you struggle with. Call them when you feel you've slipped or may slip back into the behavior you are trying to change. Accountability is not about feeling guilty or being criticized. It's about having someone who genuinely cares and motivates you to reach your goal. (See more in the "Mentors" chapter on page 41.)

Forgive Those Who Have Hurt You

Forgiveness is important because it eliminates bitter and angry responses to everyday life. Forgiving yourself and others is a game-changer when it comes to forming new and healthy outlooks, attitudes, and better all-around relationships.[2] Forgiveness is not about ignoring a bad action or event, but it's about getting out from under the control of a person's words, actions, or behaviors.

The "Faith & Family" chapter in this book (page 132-133) will help you better understand its importance and provide tips and tools in this area.

Learn to Sacrifice Gracefully

It's never easy to make sacrifices, but when you have a child, you have, by default, chosen a life of sacrifice. This doesn't mean you become a martyr. Martyrs lose respect and build resentment in their children. That being said, here are some things you will probably have to sacrifice at some point. Keep in mind, many sacrifices are only for a short period of time.

Personal Activities:

> You can't just pick up and go anywhere, anytime, anymore (especially if you have more than one child).

Illness:

> Stay home when your child is sick and take care of them. They will recover more quickly if they are at home resting and being cared for.

> Think of others, too. They don't want your child's sickness. Sick children also do not play well or behave well. Forgo your plans for the benefit of your child (and others).

---

2 Suggested Bible study: *8 Weeks of Love*—Lois Breit, 2017, Amazon.com

Social Gatherings:

Choose wisely where you take your children. Be around friends who value your values. Choose your friends wisely. Go to places your children will enjoy, not just the places you enjoy.

Choose movies and restaurants that are age and time-of-day appropriate. Tired children also do not behave well.

Go places that will challenge their learning: libraries, historical sites, museums, art galleries, etc. Even if these aren't your favorite places, develop an interest together—help broaden your children's knowledge. (Many museums offer free days.)

Recognize when it's time to leave, even if you're not ready. Nobody wants to hear a tired, crying, noisy child who is indicating to everyone around them, except for mom, it's *time to leave.*

Friends:

One of the bigger sacrifices some moms may have to make is to separate from friends or family members who are living in destructive lifestyles (drugs, alcohol, abuse, etc.). Those people and lifestyles are not only dangerous—they will inhibit your ability to make healthy family choices. This is a very difficult, but necessary, sacrifice to make for the care and future health of your family.

Eat and Sleep Well

With enough sleep and a healthy diet, your body will be strong, your mind alert, and your reactions rational, both at home and on the job. Develop a regular sleep routine. Try to have all tasks and next day preparations done before 10:00 p.m. so only occasional or unexpected tasks take place after that. And keep in mind that your diet can greatly affect your anxiety, stress, temperament, and energy levels.

There are many books on eating healthy, and internet recipes are readily available. You don't need to spend a lot of money or choose only "health-foods." Just eat fruits, vegetables, and proteins in average amounts. Avoid processed, prepared, and fried foods, which are full of sugar and additives that affect your body's balance. I will cover this a bit more in the "Financial" chapter.

Seek Financial Relief

Developing self-control in your spending will eventually give you more money to spend, relieve stress, and help you discover a healthier outlook on life. An "I'm poor" mentality is defeating and degrading for both children and adults. See the chapter on "Finances" for steps toward personal financial responsibility.

Choose Emotionally Stable Friends

Surround yourself with people who will refresh rather than drain you. Seek friends who teach or challenge you to reach your goals. This may mean finding new social groups or activities but having healthy friendships will boost your confidence and energize you. (Review the last item on the "Sacrifice" list above regarding your friendships.)

Changing a pattern of behavior you've embraced as a lifestyle for years may take counseling, but most often a good friend or mentor can help you attain your goals. Find a mentor you respect enough (based on their life choices) to listen to, and seek advice and wisdom from him or her. It should be someone who is respected in your community, church, or workplace and who has the qualities and characteristics you want for yourself. (See the chapter on "Mentors" for more details on page 41.)

When you begin to believe God's promises for *your* life and future, you have hope and direction. When you begin to take steps toward your future, you can leave your past behind. When you become more self-disciplined, you become a more reliable employee and avoid living in constant financial crisis; you will also bring order to the chaos of your home. These qualities all strengthen your parenting role, choices, and techniques.

Being a successful parent (single or otherwise) means making some difficult choices. Your lifestyle will affect the life and future of the children you have brought into this world. They're dependent upon you to teach and train them to face life, not run from it. The task is difficult because while establishing your own personal disciplines, you're also re-training your children's behaviors.

Change takes time, so avoid being too hard on yourself. Don't try to do it all overnight. Tackle one issue at a time. When you feel like quitting, don't! Call that friend who encourages you. Read Scriptures that remind you of God's promises for help, protection, strength, peace, joy, hope. Google your specific need (Scriptures on peace), and several will appear for you to read.

Remember you're not alone. Give your worries and burdens to God and you'll find rest.[3] God can handle what we cannot! Do not let circumstance shake your faith:

"I keep my eyes on the Lord, with Him at my right hand, I will not be shaken." —Psalm 16:8

Conclusion

When you discipline (train) your own actions and reactions, you become a better *you* and a better parent. You'll be more confident in who you are, what you can accomplish, and where you're going in life. Your children will feel safe, secure, and confident when their home has clear behavioral boundaries for everyone.

---

3 —Matthew 11:28

Biblical Example—The Book of Ruth

The Book of Ruth is about two amazing women.

Neither of these women had a fair life or lived during an easy time. But they *chose* to trust God amid their abandonment, lack of faith, and fear. This caused them both to become better, happier, restored women, establishing a new family legacy.

Ruth and Naomi had lost everything. Naomi had lost her husband and both of her sons. Her daughter-in-law, Ruth, had become a young widow. They had no money, no means of support, and nobody to care for them. Naomi tried to send both of her daughters-in-law back to "their people, and their gods." However, Ruth was determined to stay with Naomi and follow her back to "her people, and her God."[4]

Naomi was so overcome with grief, and probably anger at God over her great losses, that she actually changed her name. She said, "Call me Mara,"[5] which means bitter. She had been a Godly woman but felt defeated at this point. Even Christians can suffer bouts of depression, deep grief, and spiritual doubts. However, God doesn't want us to stay there. He always desires to heal and restore His people!

Ruth chose to follow Naomi back to "her people and her God." Even though Naomi had become bitter, I believe Ruth had previously seen a faith in Naomi and her family that she had never experienced before. She took the chance that Naomi's God would help them and somehow redeem what they had lost. She took a first step to becoming a "better Ruth" when she chose to seek God's people over a people whose gods had no power to heal or restore.

As you read these four short chapters, you'll see how these women began to find hope and possibilities after returning to Naomi's family. Naomi's faith was rekindled when she's around God's people again. Ruth's respectful obedience to Naomi's advice (her mentor) changed both of their lives.

---

4 —Ruth 1:15
5 —Ruth 1:20

The road to hope wasn't easy, but Ruth found favor with a kindred family member, Boaz. In those times, a family member could choose to marry their relative's widow to carry on the name of the family. Boaz became a "guardian redeemer"[6] as he chose to purchase the family land and marry Ruth.

Think how this compares to God being our guardian redeemer. He purchased us for a price (death on the cross) so that we could have a new legacy. When we accept Christ, we are truly redeemed, just as Ruth was redeemed and given a new life!

The Book of Ruth is a beautiful story of how Ruth chose to seek a place where the God of hope dwelt. She could have gone back to her people, her gods, and the emptiness that awaited her. However, her choice created a legendary family legacy!

Naomi was redeemed as well when Ruth married Boaz and bore a son named Obed.[7] Obed was the father of Jesse, the father of David[8] (a king of Israel and "a man after God's own heart") and Ruth became part of the lineage of Christ.[9] Talk about restoration!

Ruth made difficult choices to change her legacy. Life isn't always easy. Life isn't always fair. But God is always faithful when we put our trust in Him and draw closer and closer to Him, rather than blame Him, run from Him, or run back to our old ways.

What legacy did you inherit from your family? Was it a loving, caring, positive inheritance? Maybe it was an abusive, alcoholic, drug addicted legacy. What's important to learn in these chapters is *you* have the power to break a family pattern and leave a better legacy for your children!

A legacy isn't always about money; it's about honesty, integrity, stability, and goodness.

What disciplines will help you leave a new and better legacy for your children?

---

6 —Ruth 4:9-10
7 —Ruth 4:14-17
8 —Ruth 4:18-22 (vs 21-22)
9 —Matthew 1:1-16 (vs 5)

Personal Example

When my husband left me, and I had to raise our five children alone, I was much like Naomi and Ruth. Defeated, afraid, not sure where to turn, or how to start life over again. I didn't become bitter like Naomi, but I certainly became depressed and hopeless.

Life changed when I quit looking back, wishing for things to be different, and hoping other people would change. Reading, and truly *believing*, Scriptures saying God loved *me*, even in my mess, gave me hope to move forward. I began to trust Scripture more than my unruly emotions. Hope slowly began to spring up. I had to discipline my mind and emotions and replace defeated thoughts with the truth and life I found in Scripture:

For I know the plans I have for you, declares the Lord, plans to prosper you and not to harm you, plans to give you hope and a future.[10] *Nothing can separate you (me) from the love of God.*[11] *I will be the father to the fatherless and the husband to the widow (abandoned).*[12] *Fear not, for I am with you.*[13] *I can do all things through Christ who gives me strength.*[14] *Against all hope, Abraham in hope believed.*[15] *Forgetting what is behind and straining toward what is ahead.*[16]

These scriptures, along with others, kept me going.

Choosing to follow God, listen to mentors, and change old habits, were disciplines that developed into a fulfilled life for me, and a new legacy for my family.

---

10 —Jeremiah 29:11
11 —Romans 8:37–39
12 —Psalms 68:5
13 —Joshua 1:9
14 —Philippians 4:13
15 —Romans 4:18
16 —Philippians 3:13

<u>**Notes**</u>

List a habit you'd like to begin changing or disciplining.

What is the first step you will take towards this goal?

Who will stand with you?

Consistency

Chapter 2

Consistency in Training

Start children off on the way they should go, and even when they are old, they will not turn from it. —Proverbs 22:6

Other Bible versions read "train" or "direct" your children in the way they should go. The point God is making here is to start consistently training and directing your children when they are young. This gives them a solid foundation of beliefs and behaviors that they can fall back on during difficult times as they get older. (If your child is older, don't give up. This chapter will help you be consistent, no matter the age of your child.)

As I talk about discipline in this chapter, it's important to remember **discipline is about training and directing—boundaries and consequences.** Consistent *training* can turn a weakness into a strength. *Boundaries* give children a feeling of security[17] (freedom from danger, fear, and anxiety) which is essential for their emotional stability.

By learning *consequences* for actions at a young age, a child is being trained to make choices that won't lead to more harmful consequences as they grow older. Punishment is simply a

---

17 Merriam Webster Dictionary, "Security"

predetermined consequence for behaviors that are dangerous, rebellious, harmful, or disrespectful.

Children feel protected and secure when parents train and respond in a consistent manner. Not with rigidity, but with behavior they can expect regularly. That's why our children need us to make changes that will bring order to *our* lives, so we can bring order and security to *their* lives. (Review the chapter "Parenting Begins with You" for more on this.) Chaos and fear reign in a home that does not feel stable or safe.

Have you ever asked yourself,

"Why don't my children listen to me?"

"Why do they talk back?"

"How do I make them obey?"

Have your outings to parks, museums, libraries, or restaurants become a hassle or catch and release game? Are you constantly making excuses for your child's behaviors to friends, teachers, or family? All these issues can be solved with some of the consistent parenting techniques and disciplines we'll discuss in this chapter.

You're the Coach

Think of yourself as a personal trainer for your children. You sometimes hate that trainer who sets down new training disciplines. However, you are always pleased when you see the results of your hard work. You are now *that* trainer! You must think ahead, list the goals you want to accomplish, lay out the ground rules, and then begin to train. This chapter will list some tips to get you started on a new or improved training regime for your children.

You know your children will push every button known to man to move you away from boundaries and disciplines in order to get their own way. Though they try to eliminate boundaries, it's boundaries that give them a sense of security. You must be prepared to lovingly stand firm—consistently! Every home and child are different, but the need for discipline is universal.

How will they learn if we do not teach and coach them? How will they succeed in life if they're not trained to be responsible for their actions, self-disciplined in work and studies, or respectful and aware of the needs of others? Remember we are all born with a selfish nature. Just look at any two-year-old— "mine" and "me" are their favorite words. One of the earliest trainings we teach our children is to share and think of others.

A child ultimately chooses which path they will follow, but a parent's job is to lead in a direction that will be rewarding for their future. A coach learns the best training methods, then consistently trains to attain the end result hoped for.

Know Your Child and Be Creative

An adventurous, daring, or stubborn child will probably require a sterner hand and tighter boundaries (time-outs, grounding, etc.). The compliant child who melts from your look of disappointment needs a gentle correction. Your precocious[18] child will require creative yet motivational measures of training.

The goal is not to change your child's personality but to teach behaviors that will benefit your child today and in the future.

(If you're genuinely concerned about your child's behaviors, keep educating yourself through books, mentors, or counseling. By doing so, you will learn new training methods and develop boundaries that will help your child better listen and obey.)

Remember, each child is different: what works for one may not work for another. If you keep your cool and stay positive, you'll be surprised how many of those "negative" traits can become future strengths.

A curious child may often get into trouble because they want to find answers—as adults, they are inventors, engineers, teachers, researchers, electricians.

A daydreamer may not pay attention to you or their teachers because they are focused on details and creative thoughts—as adults, they are writers, artists, musicians.

The ever-playful child may not think ahead, may take risks, or do things that seem foolish. They are guileless, innocent, and not in a rush to grow up—as adults, they tend to be outgoing,

---

18 Merriam Webster Dictionary, "Precocious", exhibiting mature qualities at an early age.

happy, and fun to be around. Their adaptability causes them to thrive in many settings.

A confident or precocious child is often very intelligent and sure they are always right, fighting for justice (as seen through their eyes)—as adults, they are leaders, CEO's, lawyers, presidents!

Work to recognize and understand your child's unique personality and motives. Then you can better coach, discipline, and train them. Train the negative aspect of their personality so it becomes an asset instead of trying to change the unchangeable (personality).

Start Early

The earlier you start, the easier the training is. Children do not like to change old habits any more than adults do. The sooner you can teach them good habits the more natural it will be for them to keep them. Don't despair if your children are older—training is still possible. It may take more time and work—but it's well worth the effort. You can't go back, but you can move forward with better techniques. Don't try to attack every bad habit at once. Just start to change one habit at a time *consistently*.

Establish Consistency

Consistency is the key to making discipline work. This is true for adults, and it's also true for your children.

Here are a few thoughts on how to become and remain consistent in your discipline (training):

Never threaten a consequence you cannot follow through with.

Let your child know what specific consequence to expect when they disobey (the punishment they will receive or privilege they will lose).

Avoid continuously repeating a "threat", even if you intend to follow through— just take action.

Give them one warning only, with a reminder of the consequence that will follow if they don't obey. This keeps the argument short, and the frustration level low for everybody.

You must follow through *every time* with your chosen consequence.

You can't let your children get away with something because you don't want to get up off the couch, out of your bed, off the phone, away from your book, or leave your project.

Follow through with your designated consequence, even when you're not at home or it's inconvenient for you! You may have to leave a restaurant, theater, friend's home, or even change planned personal activities. It should only take a couple of these drastic measures (leaving early) for them to learn you mean what you say. Consistency is the only way discipline works—especially when you are first initiating it.

When I began this "one warning" method with my kids, I actually made a list and posted it on our refrigerator. The list had their name followed by their individual consequence for bad behaviors, words, or acts of disobedience. They knew what to expect and I no longer punished randomly and unfairly. The pre-established consequence fit the age and interest of each child.

When I gave them their one warning, I would also explain they were making a choice—one that would give them either a reward or a punishment. In the beginning, I would point to their name with their designated consequence (after they'd had one warning). I would say, "You can choose to obey (not talk back, be kind—whatever the issue was) and continue to play, or you can choose this consequence." Once they knew I was going to follow through, their choices got much better! You can ease up on the "one rule" once behaviors have improved. However, if they begin to push boundaries, return to the "one rule" discipline.

You know your children better than anyone else. You will know what will motivate them to listen to you. It might be taking away a privilege such as watching TV, going to a friend's home, having a friend over, playing with their specifically loved toy—whatever it is they love to do or want to do. Knowing they will lose that privilege for a time will motivate them, but only if you follow through after *one warning every time.*

Remember, consistency is your power tool. You'll be surprised at the results you'll see the first week if you remain consistent. Children learn quickly when *you* follow through.

Goals

These are just a few goals to get you started on your own list. But consistent training should result in improving some of the following characteristics in your children.

They become better listeners and decision makers when they learn about choices and consequences.

They will understand activities are a privilege (to be earned, kept, or lost).

They will experience calm, rational behavior from their parent.

Anger and frustration will be minimized when they know what to expect from you for their behaviors.

The one warning rule quashes battles and their attempts to wear you down until you give in to their "demands" or tantrums.

A few days of *total consistent behavior on your part* will very quickly bring a changed attitude and behavior on their part.

Consistent and Fair Discipline

Your choice of consequences should be well thought out, not spur of the moment. This will enable consistency on your part, and they will know what to expect.

Choose consequences that are appropriate for the action, and their age.

Age appropriate time frames: three or four minutes to a little one is the same as an hour or more to an older child.

Start small in time or allotment. This gives you room to grow if they become stubborn in their response. An hour can grow to two, and so on, but a day gives little room for growth.

Calm yourself before executing a consequence for extreme behavior from your older children. The heat of a battle is not always the best time for a punishment choice. You may need to send them to their room until you are able to calmly and rationally issue the consequence that fits the action. This time gives *you* the opportunity to think clearly and *them* the time to more calmly receive the consequence for their action.

One day, before instituting the One Warning Rule or calming techniques, my oldest son and I argued until his punishment had escalated to a week-long grounding. It was punishment beyond the action, it was done in anger and frustration, and we both suffered. I definitely learned my lesson for the need to calm myself before engaging in an escalating battle.

Be loving but be in control. You are the parent—stay in charge

Let your child know you love them even when they misbehave or do inappropriate things.

Give a *simple* explanation for why they are being punished, other than you're mad at them. Whatever their age level, *briefly* explain your reason for punishing. It's not a discussion up for debate, it's a parent spelling out the "misdeed".

Toddlers need very little explanation. Their brain synapses have not developed enough to understand your well-intended but lengthy dialogue or explanations.

Children 4 to 5 years old require more explanation but not debates.

Children can become frustrated or disrespectful when parents give lengthy discussions every time their child misbehaves.

You weaken your role as parent/leader when you debate or discuss at length your decisions with young children. You can be firm in your decisions, brief with your explanations, and yet kind with your words.

Children do not respect parents whom they consider weak; balance a simple explanation without coddling—they are being punished for a reason. Children also learn to manipulate when parents give them power to discuss and, challenge or even change the parent's decision. (It's ok to admit when you're wrong, but this should be the rare exception, not the rule.)

Do not feel guilt when punishing your child; you are training them to be respectful, likeable children who will grow into respectful, likeable adults. To develop and mature, they must learn all behaviors are not appropriate, excuses are not always acceptable, and there will be consequences for their poor choices (even as adults). An undisciplined child often becomes a self-absorbed, entitled, disrespectful teen, and—eventually—adult.

Public Behavior

Every parent wants to enjoy going various places with their children. However, unruly children can quickly ruin any outing. Consistent discipline cannot stop in the home; you must follow through outside the home, as well. If you can't maintain control at home, children will push to get their way when out in public as well.

If outings have become something to avoid or dread, begin with one behavior you'd like to change. I'll list below a few suggestions that may help you change some of these behaviors.

All changes take time, but as I've emphasized, consistency will speed up this process.

(There are more tips in the "Respect & Trust" chapter on page 61 on disciplines for public places.)

Consistent Response to Tantrums

A tantrum is whatever disruptive means children use to be in control or get their way.

For Toddlers and Preschoolers: First recognize if your child is tired, hungry or ill. These are all a recipe for outbursts from the littles. You may need to cancel an outing or cut it short if your child is overly tired. Don't put them in a position of stress when they are not physically or emotionally able to cope. There are also times they've just become overwhelmed by a long day with too much commotion.

Any Age: Remember tantrums are most often caused because they want, or feel a need, to be in control. They want what they want, and they want it now; nothing else will do! If you give in to their tantrums, they will be repeated often.

Kids are also great manipulators, so learn to discern whether the tantrum is based on a real need, or from a demanding want.

If they are healthy but just mad, you can take steps to try and regain control of a tantrum.

Soothing is always the first step

Try to find out the source of their frustration. Is there a bridge of compromise that will rectify the situation without giving in to their demand?

Food may help bring calm

If they have whipped themselves into a state of hysteria, sometimes a piece of gum, or chewy food, will distract and calm them enough to reason. Be sure it's small enough they cannot choke. (Something chewy is not a reward, it's a means of bringing calm if they've brought themselves to a place of near breathlessness.)

Leaving is always an option

Even if it's not convenient or what you want to do. If you are at a place they want to be, let them know leaving is your next step, but only tell them this if you will actually leave.

If they wanted to go somewhere after, cancel that plan, even if you wanted to go there as well.

They will be surprised if you follow through and may try to change your mind. However, don't give in to their tears or promises for better behavior. There is always another day.

Children learn quickly when they face the disappointment of leaving a place they want to be because of their behavior. Their next outing should be better; if not, leave again. They will learn from repeated, consistent disciplines.

When my oldest son was around twelve, he complained from the time we left home until we arrived at a restaurant because it wasn't where he wanted to eat (but all his siblings did). I had told him we wouldn't stay if he didn't quit complaining. We arrived, got our waters, and were going over the menu when he started in again. I got up, took all five of my children out to the car, got home, dropped him off, and returned to the restaurant with his siblings. (We all would have stayed home if he hadn't been old enough to leave alone.) There was never another on-going tantrum from any of my kids when we went somewhere again. They had learned that if I said we would leave, they knew I meant it. Kids learn when we are consistent and follow through.

It may be a great disappointment to miss out on a playdate. But if you follow through a few times with your threatened consequence, normally fewer tantrums and better public (and home) behaviors will follow. You may be sacrificing an awaited time with your friend but cancelling a playdate will speak volumes next time you tell your child this will be the consequence of their tantrum.

Rewards for good behavior and withholding rewards for bad behavior still works

Remind them of the reward you promised for good behavior, or the consequence for unacceptable or disobedient behavior. Just make sure you follow through on withholding that treat, movie, playtime or whatever you've chosen as their reward for good behavior.

Let them cry it out

Sometimes there's just no reasoning with them. However, they should definitely lose a privilege or reward for this behavior. If you're home, let them cry in their room and not disrupt the entire family. They can come out whenever they're done crying.

Screaming and crying are two different reactions

Screaming is defiance and rebellion; crying is disappointment, hurt feelings, or pain.

They must learn behaviors have consequences or they will continue to fight for control both at home and during your outings.

Stay calm and stay in control of *your* actions and reactions during tantrums. Avoid mimicking their yelling or out of control behavior. (See the "Develop Calm Reactions" section of "Parenting Begins with You" on pages 13-14 for more self-calming tips.)

Routines and Disciplines That Develop Positive Results

The following ideas are to get you thinking about ways to develop new, consistent family habits. If you did not have these patterns growing up, they'll be good to establish now for the future of your children.

Encourage Reading

Read to your children from the time they are tiny. Even when they're old enough to read themselves, kids enjoy a good story being read to them.

When your child develops a love for books, their school experience will be much easier and more successful.

Spend time at your local library, attend library special events, or browse a new book section with your child.

Take Time to Play with Your Children

In the rush of schedules and trying to maintain our own life, we can miss out on those special times of laughter. Obsessive cleaning can be very frustrating for your children, and a constantly messy home can cause stress to a child who needs order. Find the balance for everyone's well-being!

Cook Together

It's a great way to have natural conversations with your kids. They will enjoy trying new recipes and tasting the fruits of their labor.

Let them search for a new dinner menu or dessert that you can make together. I know you won't have time to do this daily but make it a special time.

Expose Your Children to Local Cultural Events

Find historic venues, explore local history together, and visit local theaters (not movie theaters).

With the internet so readily available, you can do a search for upcoming events that are free or that fit your budget.

When family members ask what you want for Christmas, suggest seasonal passes to city museums, parks, or other places of interest.

Teach Your Kids to Swim

If you can't swim—learn together!

Have A Game or Movie Night

Take turns picking games or movies but remember to focus on your children during this time.

Movie nights are fun, but there is no interaction or conversation involved with watching a movie. When having a movie night, discuss the movie's highs and lows, as well as the moral of the story or characters. These conversations help build stronger connections with your children and are great teaching opportunities.

Teach Communications Skills

Relationships are important for life, and we must train our children how to work, play, and converse with others. There is more on this topic in the "Communication" chapter (page 49), but begin to develop simple conversational routines for your family

In our current culture of social media and texting, real conversations are becoming rare. If you're shy, lack conversational skills, or are a poor communicator, look for books online or at your library on "conversation starters". This will help you develop more natural, flowing conversations between you and your children; and your children will in turn develop conversational skills of their own.

Let Past Mistakes Be Buried

Don't keep bringing them up. Always look forward with your kids, not back.

I know this sounds like a lot of work, especially at first, and it is. But you will see a marked change in behavior and attitudes once you begin the challenge of disciplining yourself and your children in healthy lifestyles. Daily living will become smoother, outings more enjoyable, and your home much happier when there are boundaries, routines, love, playtime, and stability.

A well-behaved child doesn't just happen. Someone has worked hard to teach and train them to know right from wrong, danger from safety, kindness over ridicule, and love over anger or hatred. Children are a joy when you choose to do the necessary work to enjoy them.

Conclusion

Consistency is work. It means changing patterns, but the result is a much happier home. Continue to learn, grow, and change with the aging and maturing of your children. Parenting is much more fun when disciplines (living patterns) have been established that cause mutual love and respect.

(See Chapter 13 "Parenting Extras" Teens section on page 193, for more teen discipline helps.)

Biblical Example—2 Timothy

The book 2 Timothy gives us a glimpse of a man who was raised and trained in faith by his mother and grandmother. They put Timothy on the right path from a young age. He was prepared to learn and succeed in life even before he met the Apostle Paul, who became his ministry teacher and mentor. Timothy went on to become a great evangelist, preacher, and church planter.

Timothy was a confident, teachable, and equipped young man, because of his early *training as a child.*

The Apostle Paul describes Timothy's training from infancy, and how it would impact his future.[19] I'm sure Timothy wasn't a perfect child, but Paul recognized his *character* when first meeting this young man.[20]

Timothy made mistakes but wasn't intimidated by those around him. He accepted correction, continued to learn, and became a great leader because of his early training and faith in God.[21]

Personal Illustration

Years ago, I purchased a small condo from a couple who had no children. When the purchase was complete, they showed me the home behind our condo complex which they had wanted to buy. They said they had yearned to own that home and had even asked if the family wanted to sell it. They loved the manicured lawn, the gardens, the meticulously trimmed bushes and beautiful flowers. They were sad the home hadn't been for sale. But then they told me how excited they were about the house they had found to purchase. We closed on the condo and they moved into their new home on a Friday afternoon.

Two weeks later, I saw our realtor walking in the neighborhood. I thanked him again for helping me find my condo and asked how the former owners liked their new home. He just shook his head and told me what had happened. The couple had moved into their home that Friday night and had called him the following

---

19 —2 Timothy 1:5
20 —2 Timothy 3:14-17
21 —1 Timothy 4:12

week to ask if he'd list their new house. They said it was just too much work.

They had grown used to the ease of condo life (kind of like life before children). They could canoe, bike, jog, and play anytime they wanted with a condo. They decided in one weekend of yard work that what they had admired in home ownership just wasn't worth the work or the sacrifice it required.

A great looking yard doesn't "just happen." Someone studied and followed through on the best methods and times to plant, trim and fertilize. God has given us a book to study as well. The Bible will teach us how to care for our children so they too will blossom and reach their full potential and beauty. Anything of value comes with a price. Great kids are the result of sacrifice and work on the part of someone.

You may not be in the garden of your choosing, but you can choose how your garden will grow.

Notes

In what area(s) do you most want to become consistent with your children?

List some steps you can take to begin this process—and check one step that you will begin this week.

Mentors

Chapter 3

Mentors

As iron sharpens iron, so a friend sharpens a friend.
  —Proverbs 27:17

This scripture emphasizes the fact we need each other to improve our skills and attitudes. Words of affirmation or wisdom from friends and experienced parents are emotional strength builders. Just having someone to bounce ideas off can impact parenting decisions. In short, we need a good friend on our side. Single moms especially need friends who will tell her she is doing a good job, her kids will be ok, and she's not losing her mind.

Amid stressful situations, it's easy to believe you can't do anything right, or the cards are always stacked against you. When you have these thoughts, you need a friend to speak life and truth into your life.

Begin to look for a trusted person with whom to share your thoughts or fears; someone who will listen without judgement, can give you sound advice, and who will then let you know that this too will pass. Affirmation can go a long way in bringing hope and possibilities into difficult situations.

What to Look for In a Mentor

The definition for mentor is a trusted counselor, guide or experienced advisor.[22]

Experienced Mentor

Look for someone who has experience raising children and whose children are doing well in life. You're not looking for a perfect person or perfectionism, but for someone who has walked through life and has something solid and positive to share with you.

You may have more than one mentor. You may need someone to mentor you with your finances, or discipline, or cooking. One person may have experience in all these areas, but often it takes more than one mentor to learn new habits, give new ideas, and to share your burdens.

Hopefully you can find at least one older person or couple who can speak into your life; someone you trust, someone who has your best interest at heart, and someone who has time to invest in mentoring. A person who can be honest, without being hurtful. A person with a wide variety of life experiences.

Faith Mentor

A Christian mentor can share life-giving Scriptures with you and remind you of the promises of God. Promises for good, that God loves you and hasn't forgotten about you. Promises for a future, for peace, for hope and for possibilities.

If you are involved in a church, begin to attend women's meetings or small groups where you can get to know people on a more intimate level. Then you'll begin to recognize the person(s) you'd like involved in your daily life. You'll see how their family functions. (Is it the way you want your family to function?). You'll see how they handle problems, family relationships, the words they speak, and more.

Scripture Mentor

Reading scriptures, especial the Psalms, is a good place to

22 Merriam Webster Dictionary "Mentor"

find hope and scriptural guidance. Most of the Psalms were written by King David. He was a man who had a lot of ups and downs, but he always trusted God would get him through to a place of victory in his situation. David listened to Nathan (a prophet and mentor) when he began to wander from

Godly choices. Some of David's problems were brought on by himself, but many were unfair actions or words spoken against him. He continued to praise God, love God, seek God, and repent before God throughout his life. We all make mistakes, but God offers restoration, not condemnation.[23] When you have a relationship with God, He can guide you into new perspectives and possibilities.

Mentor Expectations

You must let them know you don't expect them to watch your kids or make all your decisions. You just want someone who cares enough about you and your family to invest in teaching or training you in areas you desire to strengthen. A mentor can be any age, but usually an older person or couple has the experience you need and the time to give to a mentoring situation. Your mentor isn't there to make your decisions, or take on your responsibilities, or to control you. Establish good boundaries to begin with so that you're both comfortable and they don't burn out or feel overburdened.

Finding a mentor can be difficult, but don't quit trying. If you ask someone to mentor you, be prepared for the answer "No". Because so many people are overwhelmed themselves, don't take a no personally, but continue to seek out another person.

I had several mentors along my parenting journey. I've also mentored other moms. However, I remember when a friend asked me to mentor her. I didn't want to hurt this friend, so I said I would. However, about two weeks later I realized I just couldn't properly mentor anybody at that stage of my life. I went back to the person and said I couldn't do it and explained why. She was more than disappointed; she was actually mad at me. She took it personally, or felt I'd let her down—I'm not sure which (maybe both). However, I was in the process of changing jobs,

---

23 —Romans 8:1

moving, and was under a lot of my own family stress. I knew I couldn't give her the time she'd need. Even after explaining this, she didn't talk to me, and avoided me for a very long time. Sometimes, a "no" has nothing to do with you, but with another's life and schedule.

Glean from Your Mentor; Don't Duplicate

Learn as much as you can from your mentor. They won't be perfect, however if you've chosen well, they should have more good advice than bad. You will not have to replicate everything they say or do, but listen, learn, and glean things that will be a benefit to your family.

I had an older couple that mentored me. It was a natural friendship that developed through a small group which I had joined. I watched, I listened, and I said very little in that group until I felt safe. Gradually, I felt comfortable enough to ask personal questions from the couple who lead the group. Over time, our relationship grew to a place of deep trust where I felt I could share my inmost fears, children's issues, and life goals. They encouraged, praised, taught, and prayed me through many difficult decisions and issues. I needed them less as the years went by, but our friendship continued and grew stronger. I had many other women who mentored me in different areas over the years. Some knew they were mentors. Others I just *quietly observed* how they did life and I learned how to be a better parent from what I saw in them.

Conclusion

Your mentor may be a good friend or just an acquaintance, but they offer you relief and encouragement on the days you need it most. Mentors care enough to invest in the life of others. You may one day be a mentor yourself to another struggling mom and her family. Pass on what you've learned and bless another family with your knowledge.

Biblical Example—I Kings 19:19-21, and 2 Kings 2:9

This is the story of the Elīsha and his mentor Elijah.

Elisha knew of the prophetic ministry and miracles that had followed Elijah. When Elijah invited him to follow and learn from him, Elisha did so *without hesitation*. He slaughtered his oxen and burned his yoke. Elisha had no plans to look back and wanted to *leave no door open to return to his old way of living*. He was going forward, learning new ways, taking new steps, and finding a new future. Elisha's only request from Elijah as the mantle of ministry was passed from older to the younger was for a double portion of God's spirit.

Elisha surpassed Elijah by doing twice the miracles. The younger had gleaned all he could from his mentor and then went on to accomplish even greater things.

This is what a true mentor should desire, and what a mentee should hope for.

Personal Example

My friend Angela was a single mom who needed a friend, an example, a mentor. She observed how Lily, her potential mentor, treated her family, friends, and those with whom she worked. Angela had great respect for Lily and finally asked if she would officially mentor her. Lily gladly shared her experience and knowledge with Angela. Angela's ability to listen, learn, and let go of old habits changed her life dramatically. Angela developed a ministry that far exceeded Lily's expectations. Lily never showed envy, only joy and pleasure that she was able to help Angela overcome many obstacles and become a blessing to others.

A healthy mentee is satisfied to grow in wisdom and knowledge, just as a healthy mentor (like Lily or Elijah) is willing to share a double portion of their knowledge with another.

Now we don't all have to become great or famous people. But for your family, desire to be great in knowledge, training, love, and vision.

Notes

In what area do you feel you may need or would like to have a mentor?

Do you currently know someone who could fill that role?

If not, where could you begin to look? (Suggestions: a church small group, your workplace, your family, a neighbor, etc.)

Communication

Chapter 4

Communication

Everyone should be quick to listen, slow to speak and slow to become angry —James 1:19

This scripture sums up a healthy mode of communication in just a few simple words. Listen quickly and speak or respond slowly. If only we could discipline ourselves in this skill, we'd avoid a lot of hurt feelings and have much fewer words we'd like to take back.

Communication simply means "transmitting or conveying information."[24] When this facet of a relationship is missing, the relationship becomes stagnant or even broken.

By communicating on a regular basis, you're letting your children know you care about their thoughts, interests, and goals. It also reinforces trust and the belief you'll always listen—even if you don't always agree.

It's good to discuss your values, world views, family history (tell your story), and your faith. But it's just as important to engage them in conversations about their views. Learn to listen and

---

24 Merriam Webster Dictionary, "Communication"

discuss differences without arguing because discussions aren't about winning or losing—they're about sharing information and thoughts.

We communicate in many ways: our eyes, our tone, and our words; with volume and with music. We are always communicating. The reason social media is causing the breakdown of communication is because it lacks those emotions. Some texts can express emotion, but misinterpretation comes without eye contact or voice inflection. An emoji is nice, but it's missing the personal inflection only spoken words can express.

Create Communication Times

Create opportunities for discussions. Turning off the TV and removing phones during meals is a good first step. Then, be prepared to engage your children in a conversation so you don't have twenty minutes of silence. Talk about their interests (even if they don't interest you).

Go for a one-on-one walk. Take them out for ice cream, soda, or a meal in a quiet atmosphere void of distractions or interruptions. If you do this regularly, especially when there are no problems, this will be established as a safe place to talk when there are problems.

Communication Growth

Depth of conversations obviously change as your child grows. However, communication starts as early as their birth, even while in the womb.

An infant is soothed by your voice, even though they cannot understand the words. The tone or volume of your voice makes a difference—quiet and calm or loud and frightening. Your infant communicates by crying, cooing, or laughing. As your child grows, their desire to communicate grows. They mimic your words as they try to please you or communicate their needs.

The need for communication is natural, but it requires training and nurturing to properly express emotions or needs in a non-harmful or offensive way.

Begin when they are young so communication is a natural part of your relationship. This comes from quiet times with your child. Reading, talking, and praying before bed is a natural form of communication. Storytelling is a wonderful form of communication. Allow them to create stories to tell you, and you'll get to know what's in their head.

Broaden their world view with your stories, topics, questions, and acts of kindness.

Some personalities are naturally more talkative, others more pensive; but the desire to communicate one's needs and thoughts continues throughout life. God created us for relationship, and without communication, relationships are hard to develop or they become stunted.

Children and Teens

I feel the grade school years are the golden years for communicating with our children. You can reason with them. They become more self-sufficient, and they can be engaged in fun outings. They can verbally share their input as well as their disappointments. Their laughter and innocence make life fun and the relationship much easier. Your children still ask you questions because they believe you're smart and that you know everything. These years slip by ever so quickly. Enjoy them while you have them.

To keep communication open in all areas with your children, do more listening and less talking. This allows you to know what's going on inside of them. Give advice but remember: lectures are not a good form of communication for anybody, especially your older child or teen. They normally tune you out.

Always remember to keep their confidences by not sharing their issues with others. (See the chapter on "Respect & Trust" on page 61). If your child feels a betrayal of trust, communication will cease.

Don't forget to praise your child's healthy changes and choices. Sometimes parents only focus on the negatives that may be occurring during age transitions. Avoid phrases like "You *used* to be cooperative/sweet/helpful." Find new words and ways to communicate or highlight their current strengths.

As your children move into their teen years, the path to communication may become more difficult, but do everything you can to keep that channel open.

Your children will probably begin to move away from you and closer to their friends during their teen years. However, continue to keep those earlier conversational opportunities available, fun, and natural. Your child is not rejecting you; they are only taking those first steps toward their inevitable adult independence.

There are four little words that can build a very big wall in the flow of communication: "I told you so". Those words will never be a productive way to communicate your frustrations, or your need to emphasize how right you were and how wrong they were. Treat your children the way you'd like to be treated if you'd made a poor choice or decision. If you treat them with respect, it will encourage them toward better choices next time, and it keep your path of communication open.

As your children mature, you'll need to take on bigger, more difficult discussions that affect their everyday life—emotional issues, morals, values, and making choices in difficult situations. Ask about their fears, passions, and future goals. The more you can stay involved (without being invasive), the more you'll be aware and connected.

Your teen wants to make good decisions; however, they no longer want someone constantly telling them what they can or cannot do. This resistance is normal in the maturing process. Give wise input into a situation without lengthy discussions. (See the "Letting Go" chapter on page 159 for more help in this area of restraint.) Let them make as many decisions on their own as you can.

Choices that have life threatening or long-term consequences are what you need to battle over. If facing major issues, get all the counsel and help you can *before* confronting your child, and know where you want things to end before a confrontation occurs.

If conversations begin to wane, watch their body language for hints of worry or problems. Don't ignore changes in attitudes, grades or behaviors. (See the "Trauma" chapter on pages 107-109 to learn the signs of drug usage, eating disorders, depression, or other self-destructive behaviors—especially if your child is denying them.)

I think the transition from childhood to teen is often one of the most difficult adjustments for a *parent* to make. As independence begins its natural course, your children's attitudes, goals, hormones, and needs change, and your communication skills must also change. Keep talking!

(There are more communication tips in the Chapter 13 "Parenting Extras—Adult-Child", page 203, and "Married Child", page 213, sections.)

Listen

Listening is the door that connects communication to relationship. Parents can get so accustomed to teaching, directing, and advising that they forget to listen. Really listen.

Are any of your children struggling or argumentative? Are they angry about life, school, or family? Do you know the source of their anger? Have you really *listened* when they have an outburst? Slow down your reactions, take the time to filter through their angry words to hear what they are trying to say. If you can discover the root of their anger (or frustration), you've made the first step in finding the answer to alleviate it. **Remember, perceptions can be off, but feelings are real.** Ask them what steps you can take together to help remedy the issue.

This is a time to listen and grow closer to each other, not a time to prove you're right. Bring hope to their fears, answers to their questions, and truth to their doubts.

Because the news and information world are available on a constant stream, children are concerned about more life issues than any earlier generation. By age nine or ten, they are aware of many world issues and concerns. Their friends, (or they themselves) are depressed and suicidal; cutters and drug users; having sex; are worried about world issues like wars, water shortages, climate change, and disease. Some see no future because the "sky is always falling" in their world.

Keep life on the bright and hopeful side in your talks. We can be realistic without being pessimistic.

Absent Parent

Children are naturally curious about their family history. Children begin to ask more detailed questions about their absent parent as they get older.

Communicate openly and honestly about their family history. Trying to hide or keep family secrets will always hurt communication, and of course, relationships. Children can handle the truth but lies are harder to forgive.

No matter how wonderful a parent you are, you are still only half of their DNA, half of their history, and half of their characteristics. They are naturally curious about the other half because it's half of them. You are a whole parent, but only half of their history. The less contact they have with their absent parent, the more questions they are likely to have.

Your children's quest for knowledge or understanding is not about you or your parenting skills—it's about them. It's part of a natural desire to search and discover who they are as an individual and who they want to become as an adult. Learn to communicate honestly, kindly, patiently, and with understanding when they want to know more about their absent parent or family history.

While they are searching for answers, asking difficult questions, and possibly resenting you, it doesn't mean they don't love you or that you've failed them. It only means they are growing up, making decisions, and gathering information on a more adult level.

Honesty is your best policy without degrading a parent of whom they know little or nothing about. Questions as to why your marriage didn't work, or why you never married are inevitable; children are very savvy and will see through or resent lies. Speak the truth in love. If you've made mistakes, own them, but do so without elaborating or taking on guilt. This is a good time to talk about God's forgiveness, mercy, love, and restorative power available to everyone. It's also a good time to discuss the importance of our decisions. Though God can restore and transform, a lot of pain can be avoided if wise choices are made to begin with.

Although your children may not have a relationship with their absent parent, having a real relationship with God can make a difference during this time of searching. Knowing they were not a mistake but created by God Himself[25], loved by God[26], and created with purpose[27] helps them overcome their feelings of loss or rejection. They have a Father in heaven who knows their every need and hurt, and who will also never leave them.[28] Teaching your children to communicate with God through prayer and scripture reading can give them great comfort. Just don't force feed it; let it be a natural learning and growing experience.

I have seen faith turn many children and teens from a life of anger or destruction into lives full of passion and vision. Despite loss or abandonment, their goals change when they realize God loves them and has always had a plan for them.

Conclusion

You can keep communication open without being forceful. Natural conversations should become the norm, not the exception. This can occur around mealtimes, bedtimes, or one-on-one outings. Be creative in keeping space in your day for regular communication with your child. Always leave room for forgiveness and new chances. Trust, pray, remain calm, and *listen* when your children speak!

---

25 —Psalm 139:13
26 —Colossians 3:12
27 —Jeremiah 29:11
28 —Deuteronomy 31:6

Biblical Examples

I want to leave you some scriptures to ponder for this chapter on the power of our words as you communicate with your children and others.

A gentle answer deflects anger, but harsh words make tempers flare.—Proverbs 15: 1 (NLT)

Take control of what I say, O Lord, and guard my lips.
  —Psalm 141:3 (NLT)

Let your conversation be gracious and attractive so that you will have the right response for everyone.—Colossians 4:6 (NLT)

Some people make cutting remarks, but the words of the wise bring healing.—Proverbs 12:18 (NLT)

Spouting off before listening to the facts is both shameful and foolish.—Proverbs 18:13 (NLT)

Kind words are like honey—sweet to the soul and healthy for the body.—Proverbs 16:24 (NLT)

Personal Example

I remember when my daughter was going to take a road trip from California up the coast to Washington state with her friend from England. She and her friend had planned this trip for years. However, the only time her friend could make this trip was in early April, just months after my daughter's first baby arrived. My son-in-law had to work, but the girls were confident they could handle the drive. I tried to remind her they would be driving back to Minnesota from Washington on winter roads, her car was quite old, and her friend was used to driving on the other side of the road. I gave my advice and let it go.

On the third day of their trip, my daughter frantically called and said, "Please fly out to California and drive with us the rest of the way. We've realized Sarah can't safely stay on the right side of the road, the baby is up all night, and I'm exhausted. We need another driver. Help!"

The girls paid for my flight, and I immediately flew out to California. We saw some amazing scenery, and all was well until we hit (my predicted) ice and snow on the way home. Did I mention the heat went out in the car? We were wrapped in blankets, cold, and exhausted. Sarah sang Disney songs every time the baby cried, (thankfully he'd stop as soon as she began singing), and we somehow made it home safely. My daughter knew she had put her excitement and commitment to her friend ahead of practical and sound judgment.

Thankfully we had established a relationship with good communication skills, so she felt free to call for help when she needed it (knowing she deserved the "I told you so"). I hate to think how that trip could have ended if Sarah had tried to drive, or my daughter had fallen asleep at the wheel because she'd been afraid to (humbly) call and ask for help.

Always keep those lines of communication open!

Notes

What is your weakest area of communication?

In what ways can you begin to strengthen it?

Respect & Trust

Chapter 5

Building Respect and Trust

In everything, set them an example by doing what is good. In your teaching show integrity, seriousness, and soundness of speech that cannot be condemned, so that those who oppose you may be ashamed because they have nothing bad to say about us. —Titus 2:7-8

Respect is something earned, not commanded. It comes through years of consistent behavior. I'm not talking about being perfect; none of us would earn respect if that were the stipulation. However, we can be consistent with our words and actions towards our children and others. Yes, others, because children watch *how* we live more than they listen to *what* we say.

Respect affects every aspect of the relationship you'll have with your children. If they do not respect you, they will not listen to you and most often will be rebellious and disrespectful to others as well. This sets them up for failure in school, friendships, jobs, and life in general.

The definition of *respect* is "a feeling of deep admiration for someone or something elicited by their abilities, qualities, or achievements".[29] *Trust* is defined as "*a firm belief in the reliability,*

29 Google search "Respect"

truth, ability, or the strength of someone or something".[30]
Respect and trust go hand-in-hand.

Show Respect to Earn Respect

Do you show respect to your coworkers, family members, neighbors, and friends? Do your children hear you speak kind, encouraging words, or sarcastic judgmental words? Your children listen to you, and often copy your mode of communication and actions. If you show or speak with disdain about a person, your children will follow suit. If you honor people with your words, you're teaching them to honor and respect others.

Say your child has a teacher that is just not a good teacher or does things that you really dislike. It's okay for you to rationally and calmly confront the teacher (without your child's knowledge) on specific issues. It's not ok to show disrespect toward the teacher, especially in your child's presence. This will only reinforce a bad attitude toward their teacher, undermine the teacher's authority, and cause your child to do poorly in that class.

Whenever my children faced a difficult or unreasonable teacher, I encouraged my child in a few ways. I would remind them life is not fair, and not all people they encounter will be fair. We can only be responsible for our actions—not how others behave. I would also include the fact they need to respect the authority (position) of that teacher, even when it's hard to respect their actions. I also taught them that one day they may have a boss that will ask them to do things that won't make sense, may seem to be a waste of time, or do tasks they just don't like. But they may still learn a lot of positive things from even a poor boss or teacher. If your children have not learned to be respectful of those in authority at a young age, it becomes almost impossible for them to do so as an adult. Respect for those in authority over them will help them succeed in the classroom, and some day in a job.

Difficult people and situations can actually become tools to teach strength in the face of unfair actions. Instead of allowing your children to whine, complain, or become disrespectful, instill

---

30 Merriam Webster Dictionary "Trust"

healthy values. Help them recognize how quickly their own words or actions can mimic the person with whom they are at odds. Also, remind them people can seem unfair or short tempered when they are under stress from home, health or family issues. Let them see how treating people fairly, honestly, and with respect usually garners respect back.

If you want your children to become strong adults, able to face difficult people, teach them practical problem-solving skills. Too often I see parents interfering, disrespecting, or fighting battles that are not theirs to fight. There is a time to fight for your children, but you cannot fight every battle for them, especially as they get older. You cannot fix their friendships for them; they must learn how to compromise, apologize, and communicate for themselves. You cannot stop a bully, but if you've built confidence in your children, a bully's words may hurt—but not destroy. None of us want to see our children hurt, but if you try to protect them from everything and everyone, your children will never develop a sense of self-confidence, resilience, or strength to face their own world one day.

Be cautious about taking on the offenses your children may encounter. You may be highly offended by what someone says to your child, while they may not even notice or remember it. Relationships, friendships, and interaction can be broken over something God has already given your child the grace to overcome. If you're angry over an offense, just take a minute to consider if the offense was yours or theirs. Then you'll know if you need to confront the situation or let it go. Choose your battles—and theirs—wisely.

I want to clarify that **unfair situations, childhood tiffs, and unlikable people are completely different than physical or sexual abusers.** If there is any danger of physical or sexual abuse, you have the responsibility to do everything in your power to protect your children. *Protect, confront, report,* should be your mantra. You will never have the respect of your children if you allow someone into your home or sphere of friendships that is unsafe, or you allow that person to remain once an offense has occurred. Your ultimate responsibility as a parent is to protect your children. I know I shouldn't have to say this, but I've seen many lonely women allow a man into their lives and home at the risk of their children. Do not turn a blind eye, or deaf ear, when it comes to your children's safety. Listen to them!

Making Hard Choices Earns Respect

It's not easy to say, "No" to your children. Yet there are times you must. They will not be happy about it, they may even say, "I hate you," but their safety and welfare come before your popularity with them.

Know who they are playing with, the supervision at homes where they play, the values of those families, and the friends your teens are hanging out with. Your job is to protect, not be a best friend to your children at this stage of life.

Children will respect a parent who protects them more than a parent who tries to be their friend but leaves them vulnerable to harm. They'll know you care about them when you set safe boundaries without restricting everything. Balance is always the key.

Sleepovers are often a point of contention or confusion for parents. Only you can determine your boundaries on this.

When my kids were young, I decided to take a hard line. It was too hard to determine or know every family whose child invited them for an overnight, especially the older they got. I finally made the rule they each had one friend they could do sleepovers with. It had to be a family that I knew, and I trusted their family values. My kids no longer needed to have an excuse when invited, or an argument with me; the rule was set. We had found a good compromise. Moms, you just don't know what goes on in other homes. You can pick up your kids at the end of their play time or your teen's activity time. They don't need to spend the night with their friends.

This is just one example of a line I personally chose to draw. A decision that wasn't easy or always liked by either my kids, or some of my friends. But, I'm still glad I made that decision, and my now adult-children are too. They admit it saved them from a lot of uncomfortable and compromising situations!

Make decisions that benefit your children, not ones that make you popular, and your kids will learn to respect you—and trust you.

You earn your child's respect by respecting them. You don't have to agree with their choices, but you can always show them respect. Listen to their ideas, encourage their dreams, compromise on your decisions only when it's appropriate. Remember, respect is a deep admiration of someone. If you admire them, you'll respect their thoughts as well.

Again, you don't have to agree with people to respect them. You can have a strong opposing opinion and disagree without the need to belittle, badmouth, or demoralize people. You can vehemently disagree without hatred or animosity.

Keeping Confidences Earns Respect and Trust

We definitely want our kids to believe we are a safe place for them to share their thoughts, feelings, worries, anger, or needs. They should never fear we'll ridicule, share with others, or over-react to their words. Respect doesn't just happen; it's something you work to earn, and then to keep.

Trust is developed by reliability and honesty. If your children lie to you, you can't trust them. The same is true for you. If you lie, even in the small things, trust can't be built. If they ask you a question, answer it honestly.

I once had a friend who would promise not to repeat things that I, or others, shared with her, but she was just unable to keep that promise. I still liked her, we remained friends, but I could not trust her promise to keep confidences and therefore never shared anything of importance with her. Think about this with your children. They may love you, but if they don't trust or respect your discretion, you've lost a doorway to hear their needs, hurts, or heart.

Honoring Your Commitments Earns Respect

If you say you are going to do something with your children, do it. Eliminate excuses, and don't back out at the last minute because you just don't feel like doing it anymore. Consider the anticipation your child has had, only to have it dashed at the last minute—it matters to them, even if your plan no longer matters to you.

Your "might" or "maybe" can be changed, but your promise "I will" needs to be honored if you want to earn and keep the respect and trust of your children. Promises will become meaningless if your children have been trained to believe they cannot count on you when it matters. Be reliable.

Let your child know they can trust you with their conversations, issues, or struggles, especially your teens.

Do not talk about your children's issues with others. If there are areas of concern, share this with one or two mature friends who will keep your confidence. Only seek counsel or prayer support from those proven confidential friends. If your child/teen hears you on the phone, or in person, talking about them, their issues, or their attitudes, you will not only lose their respect but also their trust. They will *not* come to you when they are in trouble or need help if they feel you will broadcast it to all your friends. This *includes* the church prayer chain and extended family. A broken trust is hard to mend.

Children of all ages are smart, and they hear everything (especially the things you don't want them to hear). They may be in the next room and claim they never heard you ask them to take the trash out, but they'll hear every word you speak over the phone to a friend.

If trust has been broken, be honest about it. Own your mistake, ask for forgiveness, and ask for a chance to show them you'll respect their confidences in the future. If you've let them down with a broken promise, ask them to help you be true to your word. Each time you show them you're serious by honoring trust, you'll take another step closer to repairing the bridge to trust. Kids are forgiving when they see you're sincere.

If they've broken a trust, give them the same opportunity to rebuild it. Just remember, each time you or they slip, you pretty much go back to the first plank on the trust bridge. Therefore, for your part, try not to slip—remain true to your word.

Honesty is the best policy when they have questions about their absent parent, as well. Be truthful, without being spiteful. (See the "Communication" chapter on pages 54-55 for more details in respectfully handling questions about their family history.)

Self-Confidence earns Respect and Trust

If you are always putting yourself down, how can your children respect you? While building personal self-confidence, you are instilling confidence in them as well.

Your children need to believe you have the confidence and know-how to make wise choices, protect them, and plan for them. If you lack self-confidence, it's hard to build theirs. If you disrespect yourself, how will they learn to respect your choices, disciplines, or guidance?

You may not always feel confident, but let your kids know you have self-respect by not belittling yourself. If you want your children to have self-respect, show them what it looks like. Don't let people put you down but remain respectful of others when speaking up for yourself.

Remember, everything you do is a teaching lesson for them.

Conclusion You earn and keep respect when you respect yourself, those in authority, your children, your promises, and others. We don't always have to agree, but we can always be kind and respectful to one another. Trust comes through honesty, reliability, and being true to your word.

Biblical Example—1 Samuel 17, 18, 24, 26

King David had a great respect and trust for God. This gave him the ability to overcome danger, enemies, his own foolish mistakes, and life in general.

Chapter 17 tells the story of David as a teen killing the giant Goliath, who was an avid enemy out to destroy the entire nation of Israel.

Chapters 18, 24 and 26 continue the story of how David finds favor with King Saul. Then, how Saul becomes afraid and jealous of David's success and popularity with the people.[31] Saul even tries to kill David,[32] but David refuses to fight or harm Saul, because God had placed Saul in a position of *authority* over the Israelites.[33] David had many opportunities to kill Saul, but refused to take advantage of them[34] (take time to read these stories). Even while Saul is pursuing David, David continues his commitment to the people by fighting and winning battles on Saul's behalf. This is a great example of respect and trust for a position, even when the leader was flawed.

In the end, David earns the respect of the people and is made their king after Saul dies.

We are all in a battle every day against the "one" who wants to destroy us. Yet, we put our trust in God to bring us the ultimate victory. We don't need to do wrong even when someone else (even someone in authority) chooses to do so.

David followed this principle found in Proverbs 3:5-7:

> *Trust in the Lord with all your heart; do not depend on your own understanding. Seek his will in all you do, and he will show you which path to take. Don't be impressed with your own wisdom. Instead, fear the Lord and turn away from evil.*

---

31 —1 Samuel 18:8-9, and vs 28
32 —1 Samuel 19:1-2
33 —1 Samuel 24:6
34 —1 Samuel 24

Personal Example

I've had many employers over the years. I remember one supervisor who was particularly unpleasant. He didn't care about his employees, and he was crude, negative, and closed minded. I looked forward to leaving that job as soon as I could. This man did not earn the respect or trust of any of his employees.

I had another boss who was very hard working, expected hard work from me, but was also kind and caring. When many projects were still left to be done, he'd look at me and say, "It's time to go home, the work will still be there tomorrow." I wanted to give 100% to that boss. I respected his integrity, his interaction with leaders who reported to him, and his willingness to listen to new ideas and change direction when needed. He was a man respected by everyone and a joy to work for (even though we all worked hard). It wasn't an easy job, but it was an important and enjoyable job.

This is how parenting is. It's not an easy job, but it's an important job. It takes a lot of work, but we can earn the respect of our children when we learn to respect them. They will trust us when they see we are trustworthy.

Notes

What new step do you want to take in earning more respect, trust, or being more reliable?

Time Management

Chapter 6

Time Management

Be very careful, then, how you live—not as unwise but as wise, making the most of every opportunity, because the days are evil.—Ephesians 5:15-16

Be wise in the way you act toward outsiders; make the most of every opportunity.—Colossians 4:5

(Other translations say "make the best of your time".)

God wants us to use our time wisely. He knows the missed opportunities, or time wasted on foolish things, is of no benefit to us.

Below is an excerpt from an article I wrote entitled *"The Amazing Race for Single Mothers."* I include it here because it so fits the hectic life of a single mom and her attempt to manage time:

> *You're up before dawn; the "clues" for today's race will be found in your day-timer, iPhone, android, or wall calendar. You expect "detours" throughout the day and pray they aren't too difficult or time consuming. You run hard, you run fast, and you finish each day exhausted. And as a single mom you are running this race alone, without a partner to encourage you or to take on the more difficult tasks.*

Until you learn to manage your time, time manages you. It manages, or controls, your day, mood, responses, and even your goals—leaving you exhausted!

I want to get you thinking of things that will make your daily family routine go more smoothly. As you work your way through this chapter, let these ideas percolate and become useful in the development of your own time management choices.

I had been a stay-at-home mom until my husband left. Before he left, I managed my time quite well, even with five children. However, that all went out the window when I had to return to the work force *and* raise five young children alone. I suddenly needed to manage schedules, handle all the financial responsibility alone, and deal with the emotions of five children whose lives had just been turned upside down. Of course, I was an emotional wreck and was without any kind of support myself.

My days either "just happened," or I was run ragged trying to keep all those balls in the air. After countless arguments with my children, frustrated days and nights, I finally came to a place of sanity and made some scheduling and time management decisions that changed our home and our lives. I hope some of these examples help you learn new ways to manage your family routines better, as well.

Household

Being an organized stay-at-home mom meant I could keep our house pretty clean while preparing meals and watching the children. The problem arose when I had to start a job outside the home but tried to live life as I had when I was home all day. Every time the kids messed up an area of the house, I got mad (I didn't have time to re-clean it). If they didn't get their chores done as soon as I told them too, I was mad (I didn't have time to wait for them). When they didn't do their chores up to my standards, I got mad (I didn't have the energy to re-do their often lazily done work). As you can see, I was mad a lot, and they were frustrated a lot—they just wanted to be kids and play. Because my life was so focused on keeping the house as clean as I had before my husband left, our family life was falling apart around me. I think because I felt my life was so out of control, a clean house had become my source of control. Take a minute and think about what you are trying to control. Has that job or activity become too time consuming and frustrating for your family?

It took me about 5 months to decide I just couldn't do it all! I accepted I wasn't Wonder Woman, Super Mom, or Mr. Clean. I was just a mom driving us all crazy! I had to find a way to manage my time and household in a manner that was liveable for all of us. It wasn't reasonable to think I could do everything just as I had done before I took on a job.

Since housecleaning seemed to be *my* biggest problem (or control issue), I made up new house rules. Many old daily chores became weekly chores. Some rooms were always kept up, while others waited for the weekend. It's hard for me to focus or relax when I see a mess, but it had become a compulsive behavior that only added to my stress. When I chose family over my impulse to clean, the stress level lowered for all of us, and I had time for the more important family issues.

Each home is different, and each of us has different priorities, but we can manage our home in a way that brings satisfaction, not frustration to all.

Some single moms find they've let cleaning or even personal grooming slide during their stress or depression. Ladies, we don't have to be slobs, but we don't have to be clean freaks either!

Balance is the key theme of this chapter.

Choose to manage your household, meal planning and cooking chores wisely. Planning ahead and regular routines can eliminate much of a single mom's stress. The less stress you make for yourself, the more daily peace you'll find.

Meals

Try to plan your meals for the week, or at least a day or two in advance. By doing this simple task, you will have meat thawed, and the ingredients needed for each meal. This will also help you avoid fast food and pre-packed meals, which means healthier eating and money saved. There are many cheap, quick, and healthy menus to be found on the internet (or local library).

Having a meal plan also helps you save time and money when grocery shopping. That meal planning list will keep you within your budget as well as choose healthier foods for that week (or few days).

Crockpot meals are easy to prepare the night before. You can then just plug it in before leaving for work and return home to a fully cooked meal.

Trying to figure out what to fix for dinner can be a challenge on a limited budget, and even more so when you're exhausted. But by meal planning, prepping ahead, and eating healthier, you will quickly find your stress level lowering and time with your children more relaxing.

(See the chapter on "Finances" on pages 95-96 for more detailed meal planning advice.)

Activities

Be realistic when choosing organized activities for yourself, and especially your children. Whether you have one child or several, learn to choose and manage your activity commitments well.

As all my neighbors were registering their children for sports, I made another time management "house rule". Each child could choose one sport *a year* they wanted to participate in, but they would have to stagger their choices. After all, there was only one of me; I could not physically get them to 5 different practices or watch multiple events. After explaining our situation, they were very cooperative, thought about their choices, and it worked out great. They actually had fun going to their siblings' events. When you can't afford a babysitter, forcing younger children to go to multiple sibling activities can cause even more family strife. After just a couple of years, my older boys decided they liked neighborhood baseball and school intramural sports more than the highly competitive, pressurized organized sports. Even though they were talented athletes, they had enough drama in their life; they didn't need a coach yelling at them (or their friends) or looks of disappointment. When they played intramural sports, it was sheer fun for them!

Whether your family is into sports, arts, or other activities, consider its overall effect on the entire family. If an activity is becoming a financial burden, scheduling nightmare (I know of midnight hockey practices and multiple ball games a week), or causing unnecessary family drama, it may be time to re-think your options. Your child can have input, but you (the parent) must make the final decision based on what's best for the *entire* family. Be fair but be wise in choosing and managing your family's activities.

Sometimes as single parents, we try too hard to have our family look like, or be like, "normal" families, and we forget we *are* normal! We don't have to compete with any other family, their activities, or their lifestyles. Find the things that make your family happy and less stressed and your time will automatically become better managed.

Bedtimes

Having a regular bedtime for children is so important. It not only gives them boundaries on their personal and homework time; it also gives you a target for the evening as well. Children will perform better in school and have a more pleasant temperament when they get the sleep they require. When they stay up late or have inconsistent bedtimes, your home is much more chaotic. As the parent, *you* need to be in charge of making bedtimes a regular routine. Children cannot be left to make this decision.

Another bedtime tip that helps settle your child for the evening is a bath. It's calming and lets them be creative as they play with their bath toys—even older kids enjoy their bath time. (My now grown sons still enjoy a bath with a good book.) It's a peaceful time to unwind from daily pressures. Watching TV all evening *stimulates* children before bedtime. After a bath, they are ready for either story time when young, reading a book of their choice themselves, listening to a CD or streamed music, or maybe a foreign language learning CD for the language enthusiast. Creative moms develop creative children! Rested children make for calmer more productive days.

Teens will naturally stay up later, but teens actually require 8-10 hours of sleep[35] as their minds and bodies are growing so fast. Your teen should target a 10:00 p.m. bedtime, and it should not be later than 11:00 on a school night. I also advise keeping cell phones and laptops in your room overnight, so they are not up texting their friends all night (old fashioned alarm clocks still work!). They may not like this rule, but they will get a better night's sleep.

If you manage your time well, you will be able to set regular bedtime routines. These routines lend themselves to a peaceful transition for the evening for everyone and gives your child a sense of calm and security.

Shopping

Your stress level will often dictate the mood of your shopping trips. Try to relax, bring a list, and avoid contention by choosing the best possible day and times to shop.

If possible, try to shop without your children. This may not be your first choice of things to do when your children are gone, but it will go much quicker if you are alone. (Maybe because I always had five kids with me, it seemed more chaotic than if I'd only had one or two?)

Arrange your schedule to shop quickly after work whenever possible. Of course, you cannot be late to pick up your children from childcare, so have your shopping list in hand and move quickly through the store. Now you can order groceries online and do drive-up pickup. Wow, what a time saver!

If you must take your children with you, which I almost always did, plan ahead. That shopping list is your saving grace, as inevitable kid distractions result in forgotten items (and return trips). Be creative! Let your older children find specific items within their reach, bring a book or toy to occupy little ones while they sit in the cart, give them a treat (such as an apple) at the beginning that will last while you shop. Train your children to be part of the "shopping experience" by keeping engaged with them. The less rushed this excursion is, the better the experience

---

35 —CDC. (2018, Feb 5) Sleep in Middle School and High School Students. https://www.cdc.gov/features/students-sleep/index.html
Suni, Eric. (2020, Aug 5). Teens and Sleep. https://www.sleepfoundation.org/articles/teens-and-sleep

will be. Being in a hurry always causes more stress and tempers tend to fly.

I know we don't always have a choice in this, but try to avoid shopping during nap or mealtimes. When children are hungry, they will naturally want everything in sight; when tired, they whine and cry. (They are no different than adults!) Cranky, crying children do not make for a productive or efficient shopping trip. If you find yourself at the store during these times, you can still teach appropriate store behaviors. Pick out their "after shopping treat," but if their behavior was poor, do not purchase it at check-out time. You don't have to threaten them throughout the shopping trip. Just calmly leave it with the cashier—your child will learn quickly you mean what you say. Remember, you are not being mean with these actions, you are training your children how to control their words and actions both at home and in public settings.

Be encouraged—they are only little for a short period of time, not the rest of your life.

Time Management with Others

Time management is not just about us—it involves family, friends, and co-workers.

When two of my children were teenagers, they went on a mission trip to Latin America. When they came home, my fourteen and sixteen-year-olds shared a great revelation they had learned. They said in Latin America, the fast moving, on-time person is said to be "in the river", while the slower paced, routinely late person is "in the meadow". This described my two teens to a tee! My son was "in the river" always (and so am I). Always early or on-time for events, meetings, work, everything. We are not happy just sitting around; we love to go anywhere—anytime. My daughter recognized she lived "in the meadow". She was often late, she noticed everything her brother and I would miss (because we were always in a hurry), and she had a very peaceful spirit about her.

Right now, you probably recognize yourself as a "river" or "meadow" personality type. We can't change who we are, but we can work with each other and find a balance. My best friend once described me as a type A personality who loves to take bubble baths. (I *can* relax!!).

Because I was "in the river", I often ran out of patience with my "in the meadow" child. She was the last to be eating dinner, the last to be ready, and I tired of waiting for her in the car when we were ready to leave. But I never stopped to think how frustrating it was for her to always feel rushed, pushed, and criticized for being slow or late. For a long time, I thought she was just being stubborn or rebellious, not realizing the full extent of "in the meadow" personality. She was always kind and gentle, while I was always rushing her.

But we can, and need to, find middle ground in our personalities. If you're always late for work, it could cost you your job or opportunities for promotions. If you're always pushing people too hard, you might lose friends.

Whichever personality you've been given, here are three rules that will help you find peace as you manage time in your own life and in the lives of those with whom you live or work. I personally continue to work on these basic rules because they may be simple, but they are not easy.

Consider Others

Meadow people

If someone is waiting for you, be considerate of *their time*. They've worked hard to be ready at a certain time and shouldn't have to wait and wonder when they will be picked up, met, or how late they'll be for an event. Consider the fact that interrupting people who are settled in a movie, celebration, church service, or other activity is embarrassing, and disruptive in the mind of a "river person".

River people

If you know you are meeting a "meadow" personality, give them an earlier start time, so neither of you are frustrated. If you live together, allow them at least fifteen minutes more to get ready to leave than you would need (maybe more). Meadow people are not usually good at spur-of-the-moment plans. They need time to mentally plan or physically prepare. Remember, just because you're ready to walk out the door at a moment's notice doesn't mean they are.

Consider the Consequences

Understand that you will more than likely totally and completely frustrate your opposite if you do not consider their feelings as a river or meadow personality. This can lead to irreparable damage or permanently break a relationship.

Consider Yourself

When you are not overscheduled, or allow your kids to be overscheduled, you are at peace. You have time to build better relationships with one another and focus on family goals.

Conclusion

When you manage your time, time will no longer manage you, your temperament, or your reactions! Daily responsibilities, activities, and friendships will become richer and your days more peaceful. Learning to balance your commitments in a way that considers others, considers the consequences, and considers yourself will enable you to stay focused on individual needs and family goals.

As a single mom doing it all alone, you may need to take a personal time-out to re-evaluate your goals. What do you want your daily family life to look like? Then decide what steps you need to take in order to achieve that goal. This may mean dropping some activities or routines that have gradually become obstacles to family relationships—or initiate new and more beneficial routines. Then be brave and take that first step in at least one area of time management to accomplish your goals.

Biblical Example —Ecclesiastes 3:1

"There is a time for everything, and a season for every activity under the heavens..."

King Solomon was known for his wisdom, even though he made many foolish life choices. He's a reminder that no matter how wise we may be, schedules and habits require regular adjustments to accommodate our ever-changing life stages. Solomon continuously refers to the need to use wisdom to find balance, in every season of life, even as a believer.

Personal Example

I had a single mom approach me one day, exhausted and frustrated. Her kids seemed to be out of control, and she had lost her ability to make sound decisions. (Decisions were overwhelming her). After taking time to talk with her, I realized how over-scheduled her family had become. She had lost focus on what was most important for her family—peace, respect, and love. Of course, she always wanted all these family attributes, but their schedule didn't leave room for them! She needed to take a deep breath and re-evaluate her family goals.

Notes

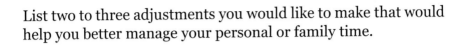

List two to three adjustments you would like to make that would help you better manage your personal or family time.

What one step will you take towards an adjustment this week?

Finances

Chapter 7

Finances

Lazy hands make for poverty, but diligent hands bring wealth.
  —Proverbs 10:4

And my God will meet all your needs according to the riches of his glory in Christ Jesus.—Philippians 4:19

These Scriptures remind us of God's promises to provide for our needs. However, He also expects us to diligently work and not become lazy or expect others to provide for us.

Financial shortages are difficult, but with wise planning and even better spending practices you can relieve much of the stress. By learning simple financial disciplines, you can eliminate debt and work towards a more secure financial future.

Changing past spending patterns is hard and it's a process. If you had more money before a life change, having less will be a major adjustment to your spending habits. However, I want to encourage you that *you can live well on little* when you manage your finances responsibly.

Whether you have a lot of money or very little, this chapter will give you some practical tips on stretching your dollar and managing what you have well.

Keep in mind, you will be teaching your children financial wisdom and responsibility with the financial choices you make.

You want them to someday be in a better financial position than you may have found yourself.

Financial stress is often the major and most constant problem single parents face. Receiving little or no financial support or waiting months for court ordered financial resources to begin is the norm for most single moms. You are often forced into unwanted moves to less-desirable locations. Putting food on the table, school supplies in the backpack, socially acceptable clothes on your children, and still making the rent is a daily challenge. It's hard to do those things with two incomes but can be overwhelming when you are attempting to do it on just your own.

I recently watched a woman go through a year of gruelling court appearances as her husband fought for more visitation with his children (even though he had chosen not to see them more than a few times in the previous two years). The judge failed to read the documents Mom provided and instead allowed Dad's charm to sway her decision. When the court order was settled, his teenage children had lost college funds originally stipulated, and the monthly child support needed for their care and needs had been drastically reduced. Dad "won" his hard-fought battle to see his children every weekend (thus decreasing his child support payments). Yet he chose to see them only three times over the next six months. Mom had more financial stress piled on her; Dad hurt his relationship and lost the respect of his teens—nobody won.

Financial stress can come from having little or no child support, legal fees, court decisions, or from your own personal choices. You can't change two of those stress points, but you can take control of your own financial choices.

Answering the following questions may help you determine where you need to begin.

What is your,

Educational background

Work experience

Emotional state

Financial base (assets)

You may be asking yourself, "Why are these questions important?" I'll detail the reasons below.

Educational Background

A good education expands job opportunities.

Education opens the door to your future. I encourage you to push yourself, work hard and attain the highest level of education possible; that may be your GED, technical school certificate, Bachelors or Master's degree. The more you're able to further your education, the better you'll be able to financially provide for your family. You will also be setting an example of determination and possibility for your children to follow.

Check with local community or technical colleges to find the best career opportunities and financial direction to help further your skills and education. There are often incentives to help low income or single parents start on an educational career path.

I encourage you not to let age become your excuse to stop educating yourself; we are never too old to learn. There are many classes you can take online in your home or at your local library. Seek out people around you who can help you improve your skills. Ask yourself, what is my passion? How can I improve or excel in that passion or gifting to bless my family?

Work Experience

A good work history and job ethic equals job advancement.

If you're unable to further your education at this point, be the best employee at your workplace. Continue to learn on-the-job skills so you'll be in a position for career advancements. Be on time, reliable, honest, friendly and upbeat. Why? Because a hard-working, reliable employee will be recommended for promotions, pay raises, and will receive good references when applying for a new job.

In past years, I've been a supervisor with hiring and firing responsibilities in clerical, manual labor, and food service areas. I can tell you from experience that the reliable upbeat people were always retained, while those who did just enough to get by were the first let go during a slow-down.

Try not to job-hop. If you can stay with one job for two years or longer, it is a plus on your resume. Employers want to train people who they will retain, not lose money training someone who will leave in a matter of months.

Emotional State

An emotionally stable person equals reliability.

If you are in the beginning stages of getting on your feet, take it slow. Avoid putting added pressure on yourself by taking on a job that requires more than you can currently give. If you're in a high stress job that you can't afford to quit but are near a breaking point, ask for a leave of absence before you are asked to leave for good. Employers do not generally care about your personal crisis; they care about the job getting done that you were hired to do. If you are unable to focus, be on time, and show up for your shifts, chances are pretty high you will lose that job.

Find counseling that will help you get beyond your grief, anger, or depression, and back on your feet and thinking clearly. It takes time to recover from loss or to change your outlook, but things will get better over time. I know it may not seem that way right now, but just keep going and don't give up.

I had a friend who was recently divorced. She constantly used her single parent status as an excuse to leave early, arrive late, and get out of overtime hours. She couldn't understand why her employer wasn't more flexible for her. I tried explaining that a business, even with a caring employer, cannot extend extra privileges because of her parenting status. It's not fair to other employees or to her company. It was her job as a mom and employee to find better transportation or schedules for her children—not expect her employer to rearrange his schedule for her. She eventually quit her job before they could fire her (which they were on the brink of doing) and found a job that had more flexible hours and was less demanding on her personal time. Neither person was wrong in this situation. Mom needed a less time-demanding job, and the company needed an employee who could meet their needs.

If you have a job you don't like, it doesn't mean you're locked into it forever. You may need to look for a new job that will better fit your current emotional level and family needs, even if it's not your ideal job. Just hang on to your current job until you find a better one so that you are not forced into further financial crisis.

Your emotional state does impact your job and could cause you to permanently lose it. If you're unable to get a leave of absence from your current employer, consider a temporary transfer within your company (even if it's at a lower pay scale). Although this is a time you need money the most, you may need to find a low-stress job that will allow you time to heal before going back into your field of choice.

When my husband first left, I had been a stay-at-home mom for over ten years. Even though I had years of administrative office experience and experience as a business owner, I was emotionally broken. I could barely get through a day without outbursts of tears. Jobs I was qualified for required longer hours and leaving my children (who were also emotionally messed up) in daycare or on their own. I started out working a part time janitorial job that fit with my kids' school schedule, and I could cry all I needed to while vacuuming the floor or cleaning a bathroom. I had to supplement my income with food stamps at first; but I recognized I could not emotionally handle a stressful or more demanding job.

Suddenly becoming a single parent is a highly emotional life change. Your hopes, dreams, and outlook on life will have completely changed. You need to give yourself time to recover, re-coop and recommit to a new lifestyle. It may take a while to find the job of your dreams, but you still need to provide during this transition.

Your children need to see you achieving again, not remaining stuck or stagnant. Find counseling if you can't seem to move forward or hang on to a job.

Financial Base

A solid base would be great, but it doesn't have to dictate your future status.

If you have a good income or child support, use it wisely. You may need to find a financial planner to help you plan for your children's future education, and your retirement. (Both come sooner that you think).

Since the majority of single parents live below the poverty level, you may find yourself in that statistic. However, you do not have to remain in a poverty mentality.

You may need government assistance for a time, as my family did. However, I was determined welfare would help us, not control us. Welfare controls when it keeps you from pursuing dreams, gaining an education, or pushing yourself beyond a mere existence. Fear can also keep people on welfare as it becomes your safety net. Welfare can ultimately lead to a lazy attitude ("Why work when I can get paid to stay at home?"). I know it's hard, and it's scary. It's frustrating to work hard and get less as you work your way off of government assistance. Most people do not jump from welfare to a great paying job. When you barely cross the line that removes you from qualifying, it's a hard transition. But that leap of faith can open the door to promotions and eventual success in both work and life. I'm not saying you're unsuccessful at life if you're on welfare—I'm just saying it does limit your financial growth, while the opportunities are endless when you leave it behind.

If you are unable to work your way off welfare (health or other issues), always encourage your children to dream big for their future. They do not need a legacy of generational welfare to rob them of bigger goals.

Now that you've assessed your educational history and experience, emotional state, and financial base, let's look at ways to better manage your money and alleviate some of your financial stress.

Creating a Budget

A budget is the beginning that will equal your end.

You may be able to setup your own budget, or you may need to find someone to help you. Don't be afraid to ask for help! Look to a caseworker, a friend who's not personally in debt, or someone with a good financial background. Having a written budget (or computer spreadsheet), not just some numbers in your head, will make it easier to see where you're currently spending your money, where you need to make changes, and where you can cut back.

Your budget should include at least the following:

A month-by-month breakdown since some months will have more expenses than others (insurance payments, quarterly expenses, etc.).

All of your monthly income.

All of your regular monthly payments along with other miscellaneous monthly expenses.

- o Rent, utilities, insurance—all non-variables.
- o Tithe: 10% of your income. (We'll discuss this later).
- o Variable estimates (groceries, gas, haircuts, etc.).
- o Look at your school calendar to know when many costly events will take place throughout the year (pictures, field trips, extra-curricular activities, etc.).
- o Savings: Even if it's only $5.00 a week, save *something* from every paycheck for unexpected expenses (car, household repairs, unexpected school or work needs).

After you've made your budget, you must then develop the discipline to live within it. A budget will obviously be useless if you choose to ignore it.

Here are a few ways to stick to your budget:

Begin to limit your impulse buying; only make purchases you have planned, researched, and saved for.

Take a grocery list to the store and stick to it.

Be careful of coupons that cause you to overspend. It's not always a good deal for you to get something for free if you must purchase two or more of one product. Even if it's a product you use, if buying more puts you over your budget, you will be behind for the rest of the month.

Define your needs over your wants. To gain control over your spending, you must say "No" to yourself—for a time. This isn't forever, but remember, we're looking at ways to get your finances under control.

Using Cash

If you use only cash, it will take extra effort to become more disciplined in your spending.

I suggest you have payment envelopes you use each month. Label each envelope for each of your monthly expenditures: rent, food, school, utilities, spending money, extras (haircuts, etc.), and savings. When you cash your check, request denominations that will fit those payments, and put the appropriate payment into each envelope immediately. Then, use the money from that envelope for its intended purpose only. If you take money from those envelopes for a different purpose, you will obviously come up short for that designated envelope's payment.

These few simple tips may help eliminate borrowing from designated envelopes:

Get $100 bills for your rent envelope. It's harder to break a big bill for smaller purchases.

$50's for groceries and utilities—same reason.

$20's for school and extras.

$5's for your spending money—you'll notice its dwindling so you will be more cautious or choosy in your spending.

This discipline will help you meet your needs, pay bills on time, and hopefully establish better spending habits.

Establishing Credit and Credit Card Usage

You can establish a good credit rating without using a credit card, but a credit card can either make or break your credit rating.

Why Establish Good Credit

There are many reasons why it's important to establish a good credit rating as a parent. Here are just a few of the ways it benefits you and your family:

You can get a loan when needed to purchase a car, get home repairs or maintenance done, further your education, or even purchase a home of your own someday. Interest is lower for those with a good rating.

Apartment rental approvals are often based on your credit rating; better credit leads to better apartments being available to you.

Many employers do a credit check before hiring since it shows your responsibility level. This is especially true for financial institutions such as banks and credit unions.

How to Establish Good Credit

It's not impossible to establish (or re-establish) a good credit rating when your income is low, but you must go about it strategically.

If you have a lot of credit card debt, talk to a financial advisor to find the best payment solution for you. A bank or credit union is a good resource. Many banks have special programs set up to help single mothers get out of debit, establish credit, and get back on their feet. Often, combining or consolidating your debt into one payment is the best way to start the pay-down process. (Look for the lowest interest rates on consolidation plans.)

Begin to pay all your bills *on time*, including rent, utilities, and any other payments. Being late on any payment takes your credit rating down and makes it harder to recover (not impossible, just longer).

If you've been paying your bills on time and do not have a credit card, it's time to apply for one—just one. Again, begin with advice from your banking institution.

If you've been living at a poverty level, you may not currently have a bank to work with. I know I did not when my husband first left.

You will need a minimum amount to open an account, but again, you can get advice on how to start an account by approaching a bank officer for help. Don't give up if you have little to work with. You need to start somewhere.

Credit Card Usage

When living on a limited income, your credit card spending must be adjusted. If in the past charging most items was your norm, that could quickly put you deeper into debt now.

The following paragraphs will help you understand the pros and cons of credit card usage.

Once you receive a credit card, please use it responsibly. You are the provider for your children, and they are the ones who suffer the most from mismanaged finances. Increasing your debt also adds to your personal stress level!

If you are on a limited budget, a credit card is only for emergencies or to build your credit. Do not let it put you further into debt with the lure to spend more.

Your credit card will help you establish good credit if you only charge items you can fully pay off when the invoice comes due. Use of a credit card should be very limited or it becomes a trap. To build credit and not go into debt, charge just a small amount each month. Even less than $20 will work.

Because the interest rate is so high on each month's balance, you can never pay off the debt with only a minimum payment each month. I'll illustrate using a 17% interest rate. (Credit card interest is usually between 17-25% on the balance owed.)

Let's say you charged $100 and paid the $10 minimum payment the first month.

Month two: You now owe $90 x 17% = 15.30 + $90 balance = *$105.30 due.* This means by your second invoice you owe $5.30 more than your original purchase *after* paying $10 off that original invoice!

Month three: $105.30 -$10.00 payment = $95.30 x 17% = $16.20 + $95.30 balance = *$111.50 due.*

Month four: $111.50 -$10.00 = $101.50 x 17% = $17.25 + $101.50 = *$118.75 due.*

As you can clearly see, your minimum $10 payment will *never* pay off the debt. It will only increase every month.

A $500 charge -$10 = $490 x 17%= $83.00 + $490 balance = *$573* now owed! At a 25% interest rate you would owe *$612.50*.

This is why it's so important to work with someone who can help you eliminate your credit card debt, and then only charge what you can fully pay off when the invoice comes due. An outstanding credit card balance will lower your credit rating, while a zero balance with payments made on time will raise your credit score.

Stretching Your Paycheck

There are many things you can do to stretch a paycheck. I'm sure you'll have many more to add to this list. I just want to get you thinking.

Meals

Cooking meals at home drastically cuts costs and is healthier than fast food or prepared meals.

Purchase vegetables, meats and fruits for balanced meals. Frozen vegetables are often cheaper than fresh and are much better than none!

Use a crockpot often. Cheaper cuts of meat (like chuck steak) will tenderize in a crockpot, and you can prepare your meal the night before. In the morning, just take it out of the refrigerator, plug it in before leaving for work, and you will have a great homecooked meal ready and waiting for you at the end of a long day. Go online to find recipes if you don't have a crockpot cookbook. It's amazing what you can cook in a crockpot: chili, soups, pot roasts, hot dishes and much more (If you don't have internet, the local library is still a good resource). Crockpots come in many sizes, so choose the size that best fits your family. When relatives, or your church, ask what you need for Christmas, ask for a crockpot or Instant Pot.

Potatoes, pasta, and rice are cheap, healthy, and filling sides. Carbs are not a child's enemy, but poor food choices and lack of activity are. If you are concerned about weight issues, ask your doctor for references on healthy meal plans. Normal meals are rarely the reason for weight problems. Processed foods (high in sodium and sugar), many cereals, soda, chips, candy, and even "'healthy" foods high in calories and fructose are the usual weight gaining culprits.

Healthy snacks will include carrots, celery (add a little peanut butter), popcorn (limit butter and salt), yogurt, nuts, and fruits.

You can also save money when you shop at the most economical stores, not just the most convenient. Don't be afraid to shop at more than one store. Try more generic brands for foods until you find those that work best for your family (including medications and household products).

There are many ways to save money and eat well on a limited budget; but fast food, prepared foods, and junk food will leave you hungry, sluggish, and often blow your budget.

Auto Expenses

Routine maintenance matters. If you do the regularly required maintenance on your car it will save you money in the long run. Oil changes and tire rotations will keep your car running smoothly and avoid unnecessary repairs. There may be someone in your church family who would willingly do your oil changes or watch for coupons in the mail.

Plan your day and errands in order to save gas. Carpool whenever possible. We all make many wasted and duplicate trips because of poor planning.

If you need a new car, check out any dealerships that may sell hail damaged cars in your area. Always ask your local mechanic to check over any considered car before making a purchase. Go online to check out the car's history by looking up its VIN number. Get pre-approved for a loan so the process will go easier, and you won't miss out on a good car deal because you're waiting for your bank to respond. Sometimes a dealership's interest is lower than your bank, always check interest rates on a loan.

Take care of your car, and it will take care of you. Believe me, I had many cars that were "junkers", but I still treated them like my baby!

This is a side note, but I'd like to suggest keeping your car clean. We're always training our children, and as you keep your car clean, even if it's a "junker", you're showing you value it and its important role in the family.

School Supplies

Be wise about purchasing your school supplies. I'm sure you already know most of these tips, but sometimes a little idea can save you a lot of money.

Have your child's supply list handy before you make your purchases. Each school, teacher, and year dictate the required items needed. Don't waste money on something they may not need just because it was on sale or they needed it the year before.

Trying to get all these supplies at once is very expensive, so watch local ads for sales on notebooks and back to school supplies. Staples, Walmart and other stores have amazing back-to-school specials. Buy supplies throughout the summer to prepare for fall school supply needs. Keep Kleenex, pencils, markers, folders, etc. in a bin so as sales appear you know exactly what you need and it's not scattered about the house. You may even have extra supplies by the time school starts.

Some schools have package deals where you pay a set price and get all the supplies required from them. Many parents say this is cheaper than shopping sales. Check and compare. Be wise with your time and money. If you choose this method, remember to add it into your budget for the month it's to be purchased.

Clothing

Be practical and realistic. Most kids want name brand or designer clothes, but you must teach them how to be practical shoppers.

You don't always have to say, "We can't afford it." Teach your children to be practical shoppers so they aren't stuck in the extremes of either spoiled or deprived. As a single parent, it's easy to feel your kids miss out on so many things, so you tend to over-indulge when you can't afford to do so. It's okay to occasionally purchase that special item, but it's more important to teach your children to think practically and choose wisely how to spend money (yours and theirs.) If you indulge, they lose appreciation. If you deprive, they resent. Find the middle ground. Consignment stores are a great place to find those name or designer brands to fill those special clothing requests (for you as well).

Try going to your local school at the end of the school year and ask about the lost and found items. They may allow you to go through these items before sending them to a food/clothing shelter. Choose generic items your kids will need the following fall, such as mittens, hats, sweatshirts, or jackets. Choose generic so their classmates won't recognize them come fall.

Purchase clothes that will last. Sometimes less is more. Some clothing may cost more, but will last much longer; however, it still must be within your budget. Purchase clothes that can mix and match for a variation in outfits.

Thrift stores, yard sales, and friend/relative hand-me-downs should be in good condition. Your child does not want to be embarrassed or ridiculed. Shop and receive wisely.

When my children were given clothes that people were recycling, I always had them recycle clothes from their closet before taking the new clothes. This taught them how to give as well as receive. It also kept us from a stockpile of clothes that were never going to be worn again.

You get the idea. Be practical and teach practical clothing choices without a "poor" mentality.

Tithing

This may be a new concept for many of you. However, I really believe in the Biblical principle of tithing 10% of my income to my church.[36] Even when I only had $100 a week coming in (a very financially difficult time), I would tithe 10% of it. I can't explain how this Godly principle works, but God seemed to stretch the smallest paycheck to meet my needs when I tithed from it.

---

36 —Malachi 3:10

It's ok to start out with a smaller percentage. Just start giving something and I think you'll see a difference in your provision. Giving to others is also a good way to get your eyes off your own problems and see the needs of others. You'll find great blessings in giving from what little you have to others in need.[37] This is a wonderful teaching tool for your children, especially in our current culture of self-centeredness.

Saving

I know, saving may seem impossible for you today! How do you save when you need every penny you receive? Again, start with just a few dollars.

When I was broke, I still set aside a few dollars every week. I would sometimes get up to $60 saved in my little stash. Then, sure enough, something would break, or the kids would need something (really need it), and I had the money for it. At first, I was upset that as soon as I had a good amount saved up, I had to use it. Then I began to be grateful for my savings because I realized God had provided for what I needed by having me set aside that money. You can't depend on others to meet your needs. You must plan ahead and make your own wise financial choices.

Conclusion

You can manage your finances well when you establish a solid financial base and choose wisely where and how you spend your money. When you cut out impulse purchases, cook at home, clothes shop wisely, and plan ahead, your money will stretch further than you can imagine. Remember, put that credit card away for real emergencies, or only use it for small purchases to build up a good credit rating. These are not hard things to do; they just take self-discipline. It's okay to say no to your kids, if you say it in the right way. (Teach them, don't just deny them—or indulge them!).

---

37 —Mark 12:41-44

Biblical Example—1 Timothy 5:8

"Anyone who does not provide for their relatives, and especially for their own household, has denied the faith and is worse than an unbeliever."

This passage in Timothy is a description of our ultimate responsibility to work towards financial provision and stability for our children. We cannot forever blame others for our financial crisis. Even if we didn't cause it, we need to seek a way out of it.

Personal Example

When my husband left me, I literally had fifteen cents to my name. I hadn't worked in almost eleven years, and we had just moved to a new city. I didn't have time to feel sorry for myself financially. I had to look for ways to earn money while caring for my children and spend that money as wisely as possible. I also wanted to teach my children the responsibility of working, practical spending, and the importance of saving. Of course, I didn't change everything overnight, but I began the journey as soon as I could. It meant welfare for a time. It meant working as a janitor which was below my skill set, but at my emotional level of ability. We didn't eat out; I didn't buy junk food—only groceries that would feed us longer. It was a long process to become financially stable, and it came one step at a time. If you never take a first step, a second cannot follow.

Notes

I encourage you to list just one step in an area mentioned in this chapter that will help you to become more financially stable—*don't put it off! No more excuses.*

Trauma

Chapter 8

Personal and Family Trauma

Come to me, all of you who are weary and carry heavy burdens, and I will give you rest."—Matthew 11:28 (NLT)

Everyone goes through trauma—it's a fact of life. Trauma is like a wound that happens when one experiences loss, hurt, abuse, health issues, or life situations that are out of one's control. Secondary trauma is also possible (i.e.: learning that your child was abused by a boyfriend or family member). As with any wound, healing may take time. Processing through the trauma may require counseling, guidance or physical assistance.

Parent in Trauma

Parenting is endless work. Little ones need constant care. If you are experiencing trauma (or recovering from trauma) parenting can be even more challenging. Wrong thinking or lack of confidence can result. Many single moms feel inadequate or like they're "bad" moms.

Wrong Thinking—a Non-Dangerous Behavior

You may THINK you're a bad mom because of mistakes you made.

You may THINK you're a bad mom because someone (trying to emotionally defeat you) said you are.

You make THINK you don't measure up to other moms who appear to have their lives together.

You may THINK your kids would be better off with someone else.

You may THINK you are not capable or in control of yourself when you yell.

You may THINK you are inadequate for the task of parenting (we all do!)

These are normal parenting feelings and are NOT danger signals. You may just need some counseling, guidance or physical assistance.

Trauma may cause unhealthy or dangerous behavior. A mom needing professional help is one who puts her children in danger while under stress. The safety of your children must come first. If you find yourself responding to your kids inappropriately or irrationally, it's time to seek friend, family or professional help.

Danger Signs—Counseling Help is Needed

Your anger is out of control; you cannot stop your rage.

You beat your children (this is not a spanking). You leave marks, bruises, or even broken bones.

You lock your children in a closet/room, instill fear, or cause emotional abandonment.

You leave your young children at home or in a car alone.

You are not properly/regularly feeding your children (missing meals), getting them to doctor appointments, or caring for their medical needs.

You are unable to get out of bed or get your children to school.

You're selling food stamps or your EBT card to support a dependency habit.

You are not keeping basic hygiene standards (baths, clean hair and clothes).

You have become a hoarder to the point there are only paths throughout your home.

You are exposing your children to violence, or sexual activities or visuals.

You bring dangerous people or habits into your home, putting your children at risk.

You are still using drugs or alcohol. You forget about your children's care or safety while under the influence.

You constantly leave them in the care of others (pass your responsibility onto someone else: grandparent, neighbor, friend).

If you fall into the "dangers" listed above, you are not in a place to safely protect and parent your children. To help yourself, as well as protect your children, you need to seek proper help. Talk to a doctor, trauma informed therapist, social worker, pastor, or family member to find the appropriate help. Take time to heal or recover so you can become the parent your children need.

A good support system, therapy, and the right friends can help you work through recovery and move into a new chapter of your life.

Extreme Cases

It may be better to relinquish custody of your children temporarily until you are in a better state of mind. Again, this is only to give them a safe environment while you recover from behaviors that put your children's safety at risk. You may be able to partner with agencies that work to keep families together.[38]

If you choose to give up your parental rights (temporarily or permanently) for their welfare, you may still be able to see your children (determination made by your case assessment). Foster Care services and Adoptive Services do not desire to keep you from your children. They only want to protect your children and offer them opportunities for a healthy future. This is a hard decision to make, but it's better *you* make it rather than Child Protective Services (CPS) make it for you.

---

38 Agency examples: Safe Families, safefamilies.org, Together for Good, tfgood.org, The Empowered Parent Podcast/empoweredparent.podbean.com

Choose Life

Defeat and death can begin to dominate your thinking when you face dark hours, bad circumstances, or hopeless feelings. Suicidal thoughts can creep in and pull you deeper into the darkness of depression.

The book of James talks about how your thoughts entice you and when they become full-grown, they lead to death.[39] The more you entertain these thoughts, the more they dominate your mind. Scripture also tells us we must take every thought captive and make it obedient to Christ.[40] What does that mean? The Gospel of John explains those thoughts of death come from the devil, not from God! Jesus came to give you life and life abundant (overflowing).[41] Thoughts of giving up or that you'll never kick a behavior or be the mom or person you want to be—are lies. They entice you towards defeat and death. God is the God of restoration. He never wants to leave you in despair. He desires to give you hope and *life*. Choose life!

Accountability

Allow someone into your life who can speak truth with kindness. This should be a person with wisdom and stability, or a professional with training in trauma recovery.

Seek people who encourage, not belittle; those who help you make good decisions, not pull you deeper into your weakness.

Be ready and willing to listen to the advice of counselors. Be accountable and stay the course towards recovery and healthier parenting skills.

(The "Mentor" chapter on page 41 has more details on mentors.)

Children in Trauma

You may not be in trauma, but your children might be. They may be suffering from the trauma of a divorce, death, a difficult move, family change, drugs, abuse, health issues, or other physical or emotional life events. With the proper support of others, you can help them work through these issues as well.

---

39 —James 1:15.
40 —2 Corinthians 10:5
41 —John 10:10

Trauma has many side-effects. Some include insomnia, anger, shame, emotional outbursts, depression, bedwetting or going to the bathroom in the closet. These may also cause physical ramifications such as headaches, digestive problems, nausea and more. Seek professional help if these symptoms manifest in your children or grow worse over time. Try to see beyond the hurtful words they may speak to the wounds they are trying to hide.

Children in trauma may need counseling to help them talk about, understand, and cope with their issue. Their emotional roller coaster will affect you. By seeking counseling for yourself, you'll be better equipped to understand and handle their trauma.

Ignoring or downplaying your trauma or that of your child will only exacerbate the problem. By remaining calm, you can help teach your child to stay regulated.[42] Ignoring issues only builds them to a state of crisis, and often prolongs the healing process.

Trauma in Teens

Whenever there is a dramatic change in your teen's mood, grades, or personality, check for warning signs of depression, drug or alcohol abuse, or emotional trauma. Family change, such as a divorce or death, can change the course of a teen. Confusion and anger mingle, causing changed attitudes and goals.

If your teen has a relationship breakup, there can be trauma.

Moving can also trigger changed behaviors and attitudes in teens.

When Abnormal Behavior Occurs, Take Notice

Drugs, alcohol, eating disorders, bullying, self-mutilation (cutting), or promiscuity, cannot be ignored. If any of these behaviors develop, seek counseling immediately.

Before you face a direct conversation, be as prepared as possible. Know your options for counselors or rehab centers, especially if your teen needs to be temporarily removed from the home. Seek counsel and support for yourself and other family members when facing these difficult issues. Prepare before confronting your child so you have answers and objectives, not just criticism.

---

42 Beurkens, Dr. Nicole Beurkens. (2016, March 3). Strategies to Cope with Dysregulation in Children. www.drbeurkens.com/strategies-cope-dysregulation-children/

Depression and addictive behaviors are the outward sign of inward issues. I have listed the signs to help you quickly identify your child's behaviors.

Depression

The following signs of depression come from the Mayo Clinic website:[43]

Sadness or hopelessness

Irritability, anger, or hostility

Tearfulness or frequent crying

Withdrawal from friends and family

Loss of interest in activities

Changes in eating and sleeping habits

Restlessness and agitation

Feelings of worthlessness and guilt

Lack of enthusiasm and motivation

Fatigue or lack of energy

Difficulty concentrating

Thoughts of death or suicide

When these signs appear or increase, schedule an exam with your doctor and seek counseling as needed or directed.

Substance Abuse

The following signs of substance abuse come from drugabuse. com[44] and health effects listed by the Mayo Clinic.[45]

Changes in sleep patterns. Either sleeping too much, or sleeping very little, trouble falling asleep, or difficulty staying asleep.

---

43 Suggested reading: HelpGuide website features continuous articles on mental health and depression. Website: www.helpguide.org/mental/depression

44 Tackett MA, Britney. Teen Drug Abuse: The Warning Signs. www.drugabuse.com/teen-drug-abuse-signs/

45 Mayo Clinic. (2019, Jan 2). Teen Drug Abuse: Help Your Teen Avoid Drugs. www.mayoclinic.org/healthy-lifestyle/tween-and-teen-health/in-depth/teen-drug-abuse/art-20045921

Speech is affected. Speech is slurred or talking excessively and rapidly.

Eyes are affected. Eyes are red, watery, or glassy; pupils are larger or smaller than usual.

Walking is impaired. Staggering or walking very slowly.

Poor motor coordination. Dropping things; excessively clumsy.

Change in eating habits. Significant increase or decrease in appetite; unusual or unexplained weight loss or gain.

Impaired hands. Shaking hands; excessively sweaty hands; very cold hands.

Skin injuries. Unusual skin abrasions or bruises; needle marks; rashes around nose and mouth.

Poor hygiene. Neglecting appearance; not bathing.

Nose and throat. Nose bleeds; runny nose; excessive sniffing; hacking cough, smoker's cough.

Unusual smell. Pungent or smoky smell on breath, body or clothes; smell of alcohol on breath or body.

Illness. Nausea, excessive sweating, dizziness, frequently feeling faint.

Shaking. Twitching, shaking, or tremors of hands, legs, feet, or head.

Facial changes. Puffiness, blushing, excessively pale.

Nervous. Excessive nervousness, irritability, restlessness, and anxiety.

Irregular heartbeat. Heart beating rapidly, skipping beats, pounding, high blood pressure.

Impaired thinking. Paranoid, irrational, or bizarre thoughts.

Increased accidents or injuries. Accidents in the house, reports from teachers, noticeable injuries.

Don't ignore warning signs. Again, schedule a medical exam to be sure no other physical or psychological problems are causing these symptoms.

Ask your doctor or counselors how to approach the issue of an exam or counseling with your teen.

Love your teen through depression, drugs, pregnancy, or other traumas. Prepare before any direct conversations and don't be afraid to ask for help.

Secrets

Secrets always come out. The timing is sometimes up to you, and sometimes you have no control over it. Secrets and shame keep hurts and pain hidden. The more secrets you have as a family, the more tension and stress exists.

Children will often hide traumas to protect themselves or someone else. Teach them that *you* are always a safe place to express their fears or ask questions; and that families don't keep secrets, they just keep surprises, and surprises are good things.

Boundaries

If you have a child showing abusive behaviors, you must set boundaries. If there are younger children in the home, you must protect them, as well as yourself. If your teen is removed from the home, keep communication open. Promises to change or "be better" must be lived out over a period of time before they can re-enter your home. Younger siblings need a stable home, protection, and peace. Remember, the child choosing drugs has chosen a path the rest of your family has not. The entire family will suffer the side-effects of an abusive member, but they should not be put at risk or be afraid in their own home.

Once again, seek wise counsel in handling the return of a teen who struggles with overcoming addictions.

Faith in Trauma

Not to simplify a difficult situation, but I want to emphasize the power of God and the Holy Spirit to bring peace and calm to trauma victims. Understanding God's love, grace, and the power of forgiveness offers hope for restoration. God is the God of

110

Hope.[46] The Holy Spirit is called our Counselor and Comforter.[47] This is for a reason. God is always walking through life with us to comfort, counsel, and restore. By placing your trust in Him when life is out of your control, God gives us a peace that passes all understanding.[48]

A relationship with God, the power of the Holy Spirit, and a strong church family have brought healing to many trauma survivors that I've encountered. It has also brought peace to family members.

There are organizations that help teens and adults overcome addictions. Research and find the best one available to you. [49]

Conclusion

Seek help when either you or your children are in trauma. Work together as a team to overcome and gain strength. Allow counselors or social workers to help, surround yourself with solid friends, and don't give up—even on difficult days.

There are a lot of great resources online for parenting through trauma or processing your own trauma. Two great books regarding trauma are: "The Body Keeps the Score" and "The Whole Brained Child".

---

46   —Romans 15:13
47   —John 14:26 (Amplified Bible)
48   —Philippians 4:7
49   —Teen Challenge (for teens, men and women) — https://teenchallengeusa.org/

Biblical Example—Luke 8:2

This passage describes Mary Magdalene as being cured of demonic control. We don't know what these "spirits" were, but they dominated her life. It could have been a mental breakdown, alcohol, rage ... we don't know. We only know Jesus delivered her from them all. She is mentioned 14 times in the New Testament as a leader and follower of Christ. She was healed, restored, and given a new life when Jesus entered her life.

Jesus still desires to heal and restore lives today!

Personal Example

Child

Margaret was divorced and had three children. She confided to her oldest son many of her fears and family issues. Matt was only ten-years-old but wanted to help his mom. A year later, Matt became ill and didn't seem to get better. His mother finally took him to a doctor. The doctor was surprised to find Matt had developed a dangerous ulcer. The family changes, chaos, and fears from "confidential talks" had taken a toll on this young boy.

Matt required medical help, but he also required counseling along with his mother. They had to learn a new way to handle their problems.

Teen

Jason was a strong-willed twelve-year-old boy, stubborn to the bone. He put on a tough, almost harsh front to protect himself from all the hurt and anger caused by his parents' divorce.

He began to smoke pot, and drink alcohol. He fought all the time with his mom and was failing in school. He just didn't care about life anymore (*big* danger sign). His mom tried to get counseling, but he resisted all attempts to accept help. He went through several years of drug and alcohol abuse. In high school he became too volatile to live at home with his younger siblings. His mother worked with a counselor to help him find a place to live, but he resisted and left that home as well.

After several years of bouncing from one friend's house to another, he was still angry; life just wasn't the way he wanted it to be. He finally began to look at his life choices, loss of family, and knew something had to change. He recalled the scriptures he'd learned as a boy, the church friends who'd stood by him, and knew it was time to seek God's peace.

Jason didn't make an overnight change, but the God of restoration was at work in him. He began to step away from the friends that dragged him down and started to look for new friendships and a regular job.

Today, Jason has a good job. He's a kind and patient man. The anger has left him, and peace has taken its place. Nothing happens overnight, but don't despair if you don't see results right away. Always keep praying, keep an open door (with boundaries as necessary), and let your children know you love them (even when you don't like what they're doing).

Adult

I remember after my husband left, I felt so inadequate as a mom (especially after being told repeatedly that I was a bad mom). I was overwhelmed by thoughts of endless loneliness and waves of great depression. I didn't want to commit suicide but had no desire to live. Thoughts of death and a peaceful place in heaven, rather than my "new reality", began to dominate my mind.

Then, one Sunday night, there was a guest speaker at our church. At the end of the message I went forward for prayer. I never said why I wanted prayer, but the speaker instantly began to pray words of "life" over me. I don't remember the words she spoke; I don't even remember who she was, but I know God's Spirit healed my mind that night. The constant thoughts of death permanently left me, and my insecurities as a mother began to dwindle. It was the beginning of a new direction for me, and my family.

<u>Notes</u>

Are you or someone in your house in a place of trauma?

Have you identified the issue?

Ask yourself these questions:

Who will you ask for help?

Who will stand with you during the crisis?

What do you want the end result to look like?

Responsibility

Chapter 9

Developing Responsible Children

"Do not exasperate your children, instead bring them up in the training and instruction of the Lord."—Ephesians 6:4

Remember, we are always training our children, so they are prepared for their next phase of life.

Regardless of the age of your children, they need to learn to be responsible for their words, actions, and choices. We begin training when they are small, but the training continues until they become an adult.

Teaching responsible behaviors becomes easier if you're able to set an example by your own daily living and consistent training. Again, I want to remind you that even the best trained children can choose to be irresponsible or make bad life choices.

Chores

By giving your children simple household chores, they are learning to be responsible for a task. When your children are expected to pick-up after themselves, whether it's their clothes or toys, they are learning responsible habits.

Picking up after themselves is two-fold. First it teaches them to be a contributor to the family household chores (developing responsibility). Second, it teaches them to take care of their possessions which in turn shows respect to those who purchased them.

It only takes a few minutes at the end of each day for children to pick up their toys. This can start when they are preschoolers. By around ages five to six, they can begin to put away their laundered clothes, empty a dishwasher, clear the table, etc. The earlier you train your children, the more these tasks become a natural part of their daily routine. If chores and responsibilities are waived for children (mom does it all), they eventually "expect" things to always be done for them. This attitude often leaves them resenting parents, teachers, and other authorities who expect them to work at a home, school or a job as they get older.

Children who miss out on this basic training can become much more irresponsible and rebellious as teenagers. A lack of respect goes together with lack of responsibilities. So, I encourage you to begin when your children are young to establish regular routines and chores, which are basic training for responsible behavior. However, no matter their age, you need to start somewhere. Old habits are hard to change, but not impossible. It just takes a bit more time and patience.

When children learn to do age-appropriate chores at home, and *help others,* they begin to think of others and not just themselves. Chores may extend to helping an elderly neighbor or baking for someone in need of cheering up. This awareness of others is the road to becoming a caring, responsible individual.

Allowances

I personally believe it's ok to give children an allowance, but not for doing household chores. Chores are part of being in a family. Doing the dishes, taking out the trash, folding clothes, etc., are all things that make the household run more smoothly. These jobs are teaching them to be responsible for their share in a family. These are traits they will need as they become an adult and one day a parent.

When children are paid to do these chores, they can resent doing them without pay. They don't see a need to help others because they've been trained only to help when rewarded. Occasionally paying them for extra jobs or projects is fine but watch it doesn't become expected in order to help out.

If you give them an allowance, let it be just that—money you determine will meet their weekly needs. There are definite benefits to an allowance. An allowance teaches your children how to handle money responsibly. They learn to save, tithe, and plan their expenditures wisely. It can also be a tool to reward good attitudes or behaviors weekly.

For a time when my kids were young and we lived on a very limited budget, I developed a "snack" allowance. Because snacks were a luxury in our home, they were either savored or devoured upon their rare arrival (they wanted to get them before their siblings). So, I decided to buy a box of whatever snack each child wanted for the week. It usually only contained enough of that item (say, granola bars) for one each day. I gave them each their snack box or bag to handle on their own. They could eat the entire box in one day or spread it out over the week. When it was gone, it was gone—and they knew there would be no more snacks until the next week. This worked out better than I'd expected. They learned to budget their food, trade fairly, and appreciate what they got. Even if you're poor, you can do things that help train your children for future life disciplines and experiences.

Rewards

There are various ways to reward your children. Here are a couple of examples.

When my children were young, I was trying to teach them to be respectful with their words, as well as responsible with their actions. I gave each of them a roll of nickels at the beginning of each week. I told them they would have to give me a nickel every time they broke one of the respect rules (talked back to me, used a swear word, etc.). They learned quickly it wasn't worth being sassy to lose their money. Of course, a nickel went further when they were young than it does today, but you can adjust accordingly if you want to give this a try.

Another suggested method is to use cotton balls to reward your child's good behavior and kind words with their siblings and parent. When they speak kind, encouraging words to a sibling, they get a cotton ball placed in a large jar. When their jar is full of rewarded cotton balls, they receive their chosen/designated reward. If they speak unkindly or are sassy, they lose cotton balls from their jar. The visual effect of coming closer to a reward, or losing a reward has a great effect on a child's choice of behaviors.

There are so many ways to train your children to be responsible with their words and actions. Be creative moms. Try new things. Don't give up!

Responsibility in Public Settings

You set the boundaries. Your children will learn respect for public property, authority, and responsible behavior from your diligent training and example.

Begin by choosing to avoid situations or places that will be constraining or frustrating to your children's ages or life-stage.

Children need to learn to have an indoor voice, especially those who are naturally loud. They *can* learn this skill! Have you ever noticed that when someone whispers, people whisper back, even if they don't know why? If you can lower your voice both at home and in public, your children will often automatically lower theirs. An indoor voice sets the tone for their welcome and stay at a library, museum or other quiet setting.

Teach your children the dangers of running in public places, for both their safety and that of others. Most of us have seen a child run into a glass door or window at some time. I've also seen children run into elderly people, almost knocking them over, definitely pushing them off-balance. Respect and responsibility go hand-in-hand. The earlier your children learn, the more responsible they'll be.

In your place of worship, the same is true. Often children are picked up after their class, but then are left to run or wander around the building unattended while their parent talks with friends. They enter unauthorized areas, can do damage, and generally ignore established rules. It's also not wise to leave your children unsupervised in a vulnerable building that has many entrances—open to anyone. This is a safety issue as well as an issue of respect for a place of worship.

In restaurants, remember to think of others as you dine out. You are the responsible person for your children's behavior and manners. Begin to train them in the basics at home and they'll know what you expect of them when you go out somewhere. Learning to sit at the table when eating (not roam around a room), practice their indoor voice at mealtime, and ask for things politely at home, will naturally translate to public settings.

It's also important for *you* to recognize when it's time to leave a restaurant (or someone's home). When your child begins to walk around, become disruptive, or are constantly being told to be quiet—you've stayed too long. Move to a park or playground if you want to continue time with your friend(s).

When your children learn to respect property, not run, and use a quiet voice, your public outings will be more enjoyable for everyone.

Responsible Decisions

Children must first be given the opportunity to make decisions before they can be responsible for them. If you continue to choose everything for your children and direct all their actions, as they get older, they will not learn how to make good decisions for themselves.

Over-protecting or hovering over your children will not help them mature, stand on their own, make good personal decisions, or become strong adults. You cannot fight all their battles, choose all their friends, be with them every moment, or make them your best friend.

Making responsible decisions is like every other aspect of life: it's a learned behavior. That's why developing this skill will begin with your toddler and continue into their teen years. If your child is already older, begin where you are. You can't go back, but you can begin training at any time, it just may take longer and require more patience and diligence.

For your younger children, an easy way to begin is by giving them small decision options. For example, limit choices (two-three) when choosing a meal, souvenir, or book. If they are not overwhelmed, they can choose wisely and begin to develop responsible choices with the little things. This obviously changes as they get older, but you may still have to help them get their choices down to a limited number of options.

Learning to be kind and share their toys with a playmate develops responsible choices. When allowed to be selfish or demanding (at any age), it will cost *them* the most loss.

Responsible decision-making skills will affect your children's choice of friends, places they'll go (or not go), the words they'll use, and their level of honesty with you. You can see why this is an attribute worth developing as young as possible.

Children must learn to be responsible for their actions and choices. When a parent constantly makes excuses for their child's poor choices, more harm than good is accomplished.

Your child may need to say "no" to one activity because they've already committed to another. This is hard, but being true to their word and their first friend is the responsible decision, even if they'd rather do the second-come-lately option. If they are coddled or told it's ok to ditch their first friend for the more fun second invitation, it's a step backwards in their training.

A person can be responsible and still have fun. However, if choices are not made responsibly, that fun eventually turns into disaster.

Because responsible decision-making skills will become even more important as your children grow, let me talk about teens for just a moment. (Children grow up quickly!)

Strategic Responsibilities for Teens

Keep in mind your teen is trying to become an adult, a natural part of growing up; remember we all did it! They are trying to make decisions on their own, figure out who they are (not who *you* want them to be), and become as independent as they can possibly get away with. Of course, in the midst of pushing for

122

adulthood status, they resist many of the responsibilities that accompany adulthood.

Teens who balk at household chores will often struggle with the responsibilities of a job, the expectations of a boss, or life itself.

The earlier they develop a sense of responsibility, the easier their transition to college, work, and adulthood will become. If they gripe about their chores, ignore it, this is part of the teen mantra; don't escalate issues you can ignore.

Working is part of a teen's transition into adulthood. I've listed a few benefits below to help you better understand how a job helps develop responsible behaviors.

Working

Develops team, goal, and managerial skills.

Covers the finances for your teen's extras, those things you cannot, or *should not* be paying for. If they never have to pay for those things, they will continue to expect someone to provide for them, not earn it themselves or be appreciative.

Keeps your teen out of trouble during those after school hours before you get home from work. (Extracurricular activities can also serve to fill those idle hours. However, some type of work is still a good maturing experience. You know your teen, and what's best for them.

Offers experience and references for future college job opportunities.

Teaches them how to balance personal life, studies, finances, and work—something they will need throughout their life.

Develops life skills and responsibility. If your teen tends to be more immature or irresponsible, they may lose a job they liked, but this also becomes a learning experience—not the end of the world. They'll discover you are not the only one who expects them to be on time, have a good attitude, and be responsible.

A job should *not* interfere with their schoolwork; 8-12 hours per week is plenty for a high school student. By their senior year they may work more but watch it doesn't interfere with their grades.

Your teen needs to understand you will not be supporting them for the rest of their life, or for years while they "find themselves".

They need *you* to prepare *them* to work, study, and make sound choices, or they have little chance of success in the work world or in life.

Guide your teen to think about their future, their work goals, or college goals. Students without goals often fail as they flounder trying to figure out life, while life is passing them by.

(See the "Parenting Extras" chapter on "Teens", page 193, for more teen parenting tips.)

Conclusion

Develop responsible habits that will better prepare your children or teen for adult life while they are young. Don't take away their fun but help them be prepared to make the best possible choices when they get older.

Teens often want independence and money, but not the responsibilities that earn either. They need a parent who will teach them responsible behaviors, which better prepares them for a more successful future.

Biblical Example—Exodus 18:13-27

Here we find the story of Moses when he is put in the position of judge over all the Israelites' disputes. Moses took his job seriously, wanted to do it well, and yet he was taking on too much responsibility. His father-in-law showed him how to better delegate, leaving only the bigger or more important decisions to Moses.

We can learn from this lesson as single moms. Sometimes we take on *all* the responsibilities and decisions, when we need to train our children to help carry the load. Moses had to find a balance in being responsible and sharing responsibilities. So must we!

Personal Example

My nine-year-old son had become very crabby about everything after his dad had left. When I finally asked him why he was so angry he replied, "I'm so mad I'm not old enough to get a job and take care of us." This little boy was taking on responsibilities that were not his. Once I knew the issue, I was able to calm his frustrations and fears. It also caused me to be more careful in expressing our needs, so this little boy could be free from his self-imposed burden.

Just like the story of Moses, we must know how to teach responsible behaviors, without overloading our children with adult issues, responsibilities, and fears.

Notes

List two areas you'd like to see your children learn to take more responsibility for. It may be their words, actions, or helps.

1.

2.

What can you do to help them become more responsible in this area?

List one or two areas of responsibility you need to give to someone else. It might be a chore, or an obligation.

1.

2.

Determine a timeline and method to make this change.

Faith

Chapter 10

Incorporating Faith into

Your Family Time

You may be asking why I included this chapter in a parenting book. It's because I've seen and experienced how faith and a church family have been key factors in the healing and restorative process of a family going through crisis, change, loss, or even everyday struggles. Faith builds self-confidence, strength, and security. Faith gives hope for each day and provides vision for the future.

Faith isn't about the do's and don'ts of living a Christian life—it's about a relationship with the living God, and the blessings that follow those who keep Him first in their lives.

In this chapter, I'll look at the *hindrances, influencers,* and some *practical steps* that will affect your faith and family times.

A father to the fatherless, a defender of widows is God in His holy dwelling. He places the lonely in families . . .
    —Psalm 68:5–6

Are you feeling alone, or without a defender? God cares about you and desires to give hope when you feel lonely, abandoned or overwhelmed. He defends you against your enemy of defeatism, hopelessness, fear, anxiety, and loneliness. I believe, today, the *church is the family* where many will find the help and friendships needed to heal.

Hindrances

But if serving the Lord seems undesirable to you, then choose for yourselves this day whom you will serve, whether the gods your ancestors served beyond the Euphrates, or the gods of the Amorites, in whose land you are living. But as for me and my household, we will serve the Lord." —Joshua 24:15

The 'Gods' You've Chosen

Your gods are those people or things you look to for help, soothing, or to forget, but which only offer a *temporary* respite, or fleeting pleasure. These god's can be harmful lifestyles, your anger, bitterness, isolation, living as a victim for sympathy, or a substance that gives brief relief to a long-term pain.

Ask yourself if those gods are keeping you stuck in your circumstance or lifting you out of it. Do you still feel broken, angry, addicted, and your home life remains chaotic? Maybe it's time to look to the God who truly loves *you*, who still heals and restores lives—permanently![50]

> *Choose today whom you will serve.* God lets us choose— what god are you choosing for you and your household?

Birth Families

With so many second and third generationally broken, dysfunctional, and single parent homes, a birth family may be the source of destructive habits or negative attitudes. If your birth family feeds defeat, anger, or poor lifestyles, you may need to separate from them—at least for a time. Give yourself time to see life from a different perspective.

---

50 Suggested Bible study: *"8 Weeks of Love"*, Lois Breit,—Amazon.com

Friends

If friends ridicule, or degrade a spiritual life, this is obviously a hindrance. Do their schedules keep you from attending church or small groups? Are they stuck in a defeated lifestyle or attitude, or keep you connected to habits you're trying to break? Negative friendships can determine your walk with God, your spiritual commitment, and even your future.

Influencers

Family and Friends

If you have a strong family support system, count yourself lucky. It's great to have family surround you, encourage you, and help you restart your life. Remain grateful and thankful for all they do to help.

Choose friends who build you up, bring healing, give wisdom, and live a lifestyle you'd like to emulate.

Even if you have a good family, I encourage you to incorporate God and His people into your life and your story. A healthy church family and Biblical teachings give you a new, clear vision of who you are and who God is; this can profoundly impact your choices and your future.

Practical Faith Building Steps

Know You're Loved

See what great love the Father has lavished on us, that we should be called children of God! And that is what we are!
    —1 John 3:1a

For you created my inmost being; you knit me together in my mother's womb. I praise you because I am fearfully and wonderfully made; your works are wonderful.
    —Psalm 139:13–14

God loves you because He created you, and you are His child. His capacity for love and mercy is so much greater than ours!

When you feel unloved, you make choices based on the belief you don't deserve good things or happiness. Believing you have no value keeps you trapped in a life of failure and defeat.

When you believe God loves *you*, it changes everything.[51] You begin to look at life differently, respond differently, and live differently. When you believe God desires to bless you, not harm you, and that He has a plan and a future for you and your children[52], you make wiser choices and set new goals. When you know His promises for peace, joy[53], and an abundant life[54], the struggles and storms of life don't remain bottomless pits, but passages to something better.

Let Go of the Past

Remember not the former things, nor consider the things of old. Behold, I am doing a new thing...—Isaiah 43:18–19

Get rid of all bitterness, rage and anger, brawling and slander, along with every form of malice.—Ephesians 4:31

For if you forgive others their trespasses, your heavenly Father will also forgive you.—Matthew 6:14

These Scriptures are a reminder that we cannot move forward until we release our past, through forgiveness and new choices.

The person, place, or thing that's hurt you will dictate your future until you let it go. You won't forget your past, but it no longer needs to control your daily life, reactions, or choices.

Letting go and forgiving go hand-in-hand. Forgiveness is a choice, but it's also a process, not a one-and-done. Forgiveness means turning over to God your pain, the person, or the event. It's choosing to no longer drag it around with you each day. When you forgive someone, you're set free from their words, thoughts, and actions toward you. That person may never change, but you will! You may never say those words ("I forgive you") to the person—only to God—but by saying them out loud (often repeatedly), you sever their tie and power over you. Their control is broken. You are free to live life without your past dictating your future.

---

51 —Psalm 139:13-16
52 —Jeremiah 29:11
53 —Galatians 5:22
54 —John 10:10

Blame, bitterness, and unforgiveness only hurt you and allows your "enemy" to remain in control of your daily thoughts, emotions and future.[55] *Let it go* and find the peace and joy God has waiting for you. *Let it go* and find the future He has for you, and the new legacy awaiting your children. *Let it go* and find life instead of defeat. *Let it go* and find the blessings of God, not the emptiness of past failures or pain.

Become Part of a Church Family

A church family can provide counselors, mentors, workers, friends, visionaries, and of course, the Word of God, which gives direction for all aspects of life. A church should be a safe place and refuge for your family. A church family can surround you with love and encouragement.

At one time, I worked on staff at my church. I was responsible for the benevolence fund, which was used to help families in need. I often received random calls from single moms asking for financial help to pay their bills. I always asked if they were connected with a church family in our community. They usually replied it was just too hard to get to church with their children. I would share how, even with five kids, I made it a priority to be part of a church family—it's a choice we make. I would then encourage those moms to connect with a church, because when a church family knows you and your kids, they will want to help. It wasn't that we didn't help people outside of our church, but funds were limited, and we needed to know where the money was actually going. Helping is one thing but enabling is never healthy.

If you've had a bad church experience, find a new church! God is not the source of your problem, but the solution to it. All church people are not "nice" people, or mature Christians (regardless of how long they've been in the church). Attach yourself to the true seekers, the kind and trustworthy ones. Don't allow a bad church person or experience rob you of the blessings God has waiting for you and your family.

---

55 —Galatians 5:15—"*If you bite and devour each other, watch out or you will be destroyed by each other.*"

Keep Spiritual Life a Priority for Your Family

As long as you keep God first, sports, work, and other activities will align. However, if those activities are pulling your family away from God and your spiritual growth, rather than closer, it may be time to re-evaluate your priorities. Words, actions, and attitudes are a great indicator of your family's spiritual life.

There are many student jobs that will leave your teen free to attend youth nights and Sunday services. The same is true for their sports, arts, or extracurricular interests. What you deem important sets the tone of the household.

I knew a single mom who lived in a small town with few church choices. She drove almost two hours, one-way, to a church that brought life to her family. That may sound extreme, but people drive further than that to attend their child's sporting event every week without blinking an eye. It's all about your current priorities and future goals.

Keeping your faith a priority gives God the opportunity to lead and direct your life, as well as your children's.

Read Your Bible

If you don't know where to begin reading the Bible on your own, try the following each day:

Read one proverb as a daily personal challenge.

Read one chapter in Psalms for encouragement.

Keep in mind the Psalms are divided by what's happening in King David's life. In one part, David is staying faithful to God while fleeing from King Saul, who is trying to kill him. In another, David is repenting of his sins and failures. It ends with songs of praise. But throughout, David recounts the victories found through his faith in God.

Read at least one paragraph or section from the New Testament to help in understanding God's love for you.

Matthew, Mark, Luke, and John all tell the story of Jesus' birth and ministry. They're called the Gospels, which just means they are the teachings and revelation of Christ. They were written to four diverse cultural groups that made up the population of the time.

God wanted all peoples and cultures to understand the message of Jesus Christ. All could be redeemed (restored to God's family), and all could receive the gift of eternal life.

If you're unfamiliar with the Bible, begin with the book of John. It's the story of Jesus, covering His birth, death, and resurrection. It also covers many of the miracles He performed.

Other good books of the Bible to start with include:

Romans, a book about the foundations of faith.

Philippians, a book about joy, even in difficult times. It was written from a prison cell and reminds us to rejoice regardless of our situation. God is still with us.

James teaches about the power of our tongue, and why it's so hard to tame it.

Acts recounts God sending the Holy Spirit to empower all believers.

Reading Scriptures before bed can also bring calm to your very hectic day.

Develop a Devotional Time

Why, in the middle of your crazy busy world, would you want to take a personal time out to develop a devotional life? What does that even mean?

The word "devotion" simply means devoting yourself to something or someone. When you are devoted to a person you love, you take time to be with them, listen to them, respect them, and look forward to your daily conversations. It's no different with God. But just like with any relationship, zeal and excitement can get lost in the midst of hectic, stressful, crisis-filled days. If we don't set apart a time for God, we rush through each day without His peace, lose our joy, and revert to old habits.

If you don't spend time with a person you love, the relationship will eventually wane, become routine, lack excitement, and soon die. Loving God is no different. God desires to commune (walk and talk) with us every day. (Think of Adam and Eve in the Garden—they had daily communion with God.) We need Him every day if we're going to stay focused on what's important in this life.

I talk to God throughout my day. I ask questions, seek advice, offer prayers, and sing songs of praise. But I also need to have a dedicated quiet time, alone with Him and without distractions, on a regular basis.

This personal "time out" is important for both the spiritual growth of your family and for the values it establishes. It shouldn't be an added stress for you or deprive you of your much-needed sleep. It's just a time to thank God for all he's done, or be a reminder He is still with you—even if you *feel* alone. Use it to acknowledge Him as your Lord and Savior, the all-knowing, all-loving, merciful, creator God. Then bring your needs before Him, be encouraged by the Scriptures, and just sit quietly in His presence.

There are many different ways to have devotions, both personally and as a family. Start out small and simple at a time that's most convenient for you, then your desire to continue will grow.

Personal Devotions

Devotions are not punishment; they're a special quiet time between you and the God who has rescued you, forgiven you, loves you, and desires to bless you.

Start with five minutes. Try not to look at the clock. Instead, set a timer so you can keep your mind focused. Some days will be longer and others, shorter, but begin here. It's not about the amount of time but the quality of time.

Choose a time that works for you. Mornings are good because it gets your focus on God for the start of your day. But if you're not a morning person, try to read just one Proverb to start your day.

I wasn't a morning person—I wanted to sleep as long as possible. My best time with the Lord came before I went to sleep. Reading the Word, talking to God, focusing on Him instead of all my stress and fears, caused me to sleep more peacefully through the night.

Find *your* best time and develop it as a daily pattern. If you desire to have Him restore, heal, and direct your family life, don't let excuses keep you from this special time with God.

Put your Bible where you'll see it and use it. Next to your bed, on your dining room table or end table; just *not* on a shelf where it's out of sight and out of mind.

Once you establish a regular time, it will become a respite you look forward to each day.

Here are a few suggestions on how to begin a devotional time that can be done in five minutes.

Find a quiet spot where you won't be interrupted. This keeps you focused on God instead of the daily distractions of life.

Praise and worship Him with your words or through songs. Spend a minute thanking God that He's in your life. Thank Him for being in control, even when you're not, and for loving you, even when you don't deserve it (or feel it). This helps you connect more closely with God.

Bring your requests to God. He knows what you need but seeking Him through prayer releases power.

Read one Bible verse, paragraph, or chapter. If you're using a devotional book, follow its daily plan. This builds a stronger foundation for your faith.

Reflect on what you've read and how you can apply it to your day. This allows the Holy Spirit (God's still small voice) to speak into or give direction for daily situations, choices, and anxieties.

Keep your relationship two-way, fresh and relevant, rather than distant and one-way (asking but not listening or responding).

I repeat—a devotional time does not need to be hard or overwhelming. It's just forming a habit to keep God as a daily priority in your life. Your personal devotional times may change as jobs change, kids' schedules change, and personal needs change. But keep them fresh and ongoing.

Family Devotions

Your family devotions will also change over time, depending on the ages and stages of your children. Here are just a few suggestions to get you started:

> Read a few verses or one chapter of the Bible to your children while they eat breakfast before school. I know this is a rushed time, and many kids eat breakfast in the car or at school, but this may work for you.

> The same as above, but at dinnertime (I also recommend eating dinner together whenever possible without any phone or TV interruptions). This is the best time to initiate conversations with your kids.

> The same, but before bed. This is a great time, as your kids wind-down at the end of the day. It's also a good conversational time to discuss what you've read. Be sure to start their bedtime routine early enough to allow time for questions.

Join a Small Group or Bible Study

> Devotions are personal times spent with God.

> Small groups are when believers come together to learn from each other and grow in their faith. They may or may not study the Bible. They may be interest-driven, but most will include some type of devotional lesson with their outing.

> Bible Studies help you search the Scriptures, answer personal questions, and apply the Scriptures. You can do a Bible study on your own, but being part of a group study will help you build relationships with other believers, give you a safe place to ask questions, hear others' thoughts on the Scriptures you're reading, and deepen your biblical knowledge. A Sunday message is meant to encourage and teach, but your faith expands as you dig deeper into the meaning of Scriptures through open discussion. In many churches, small group studies have replaced the deeper teachings formerly taught in Sunday school or Sunday evening services.

Most churches offer a variety of small groups or Bible studies.

Groups are often designed for specific interests, ages, or topics to be discussed, and some are a mix of ages and topics. Choose one that works for you. If you're not comfortable in a specific group, you're not chained to it—just switch to another.

I felt very uncomfortable with the very first small group I chose. I didn't fit in, and the attitudes were not what I needed. But the next group I tried was perfect for me. I learned so much about healthy relationships and the scriptures from this very eclectic group of people.

Being in a group with couples can also be good for single parents. If you've come from an unhealthy or abusive relationship, you can observe healthier family interactions, learn new parenting skills, or let them see you are just a normal family as well.

Tithe

I talked about this in the "Finance" chapter, but because it's an important part of incorporating faith into your family, I'll mention it here as well.

For Christians, tithing is not a suggestion, but something God asks of us. Scriptures are quite clear that ten percent of our income is to be set aside as a tithe to the Lord, which we give through our local church. Scriptures also say, "God will pour out his blessings on those who tithe!"[56]

God doesn't need our money, but a tithe is another way we express our love for God (and His work) and reinforces our decision to put God first in our lives. Because tithing is a heart issue—a show of our love for God—we don't give to *get*. However, we'll be blessed as we tithe. It's a Godly principle I can't explain—I've just seen the reality of sowing and reaping in this area of faith.

If fear keeps you from giving a tithe, begin small. Give one percent, five percent, or whatever percent gets you started. I believe you'll see you have more of what you need, when you need it, after you begin to tithe.

---

56 —Malachi 3:10

Conclusion

Putting God first in your daily life will impact your decisions, relationships, and even your family legacy. Don't underestimate what the God of miracles and impossibilities can do in your family!

Biblical Example—Genesis 19

This is the story of Lot (nephew of Abraham) and his family. He chose to stay in a sinful city (Sodom), surrounding his wife and daughters with ungodly people and practices. The entire city was corrupt of morals and absent of a belief in God. When the angels finally led (pulled)[57] Lot and his family away from the city, his wife looked back (unable to leave the old life behind) and she died.[58] His daughters get Lot drunk, sleep with him and have sons by him named Moab and Ammon. The offspring of those children become enemies of God's people for generations. Their lineages become the Moabites and the Ammonites who were enemies of the Israelites throughout the Old Testament.[59]

Lot thought he could live among the pagans (unbelievers) and not have his family corrupted by them. Lot saw his surroundings but did nothing to escape it. He thought he could stay in the middle of destruction and not be touched by it. Lot could have gone to Abraham for help anytime he wanted, but he chose the comfort of his location over the safety and future of his family. We don't always get to choose where we land in life, but we can choose whether to stay there or not and with whom we surround ourselves.

Personal Example

I will share my church family story here. But I want to add, without my faith and trust in God, I doubt very much I would be alive today. He truly rescued me from "my pit" and placed my feet on solid ground.[60]

---

57 —Genesis 19:16
58 —Genesis 19:26
59 —Genesis 19:30-33
60 —Psalm 40:1-2

My Church Family Story

My husband left when our children were 2, 5, 7, 9, and 11 years of age. We had just moved to a new city, neighborhood, and school for my kids. I literally had 15 cents to my name, no car, and hadn't worked in over 10 years. I was depressed, afraid, overwhelmed, and totally confused about how our marriage had fallen apart.

I didn't know what the truth was or who I was anymore. I still loved my husband, but he had found someone new to love—I was left behind. His rejection, abandonment, and hurtful words had put me in a downward spiral. I was an emotional basket case when I *stumbled* into a church that became our home and church family. I was very hopeless but believed in my heart if we had any chance to heal and survive it would only be through the grace of God, and the love of a church family.

I'm thankful I found the right church for us!

My kids weren't always happy about being at church, especially during those first few months as we made it a routine. However, over-time they saw the difference it was making in our family. Eventually, I couldn't keep them away. They loved their youth group and the new friends they made there.

Because I didn't have a car, a neighbor took us to church for every service and every event for weeks.

Then one day, the pastor brought over his old car that had suddenly started after months of not working. I drove that car for six months without a problem. When I was able to purchase my own car, I give his car back. Curiously, it never started again for him. He had to junk it.

An anonymous church member donated four tires for my new-to-me car when they noticed they were bald. I never asked for tires, and to this day I do not know who gave them to me.

A healthy (church) family takes care of its own.

After my husband left,

> One daughter began to have nightmares. Our new pastor and his wife came to our home and prayed over her and her bedroom—her nightmares stopped. She's grown into a strong and fearless woman of God—serving youth, adults, and missionaries.

> My nine-year-old became mouthy and sarcastic to cover up his pain. He tried everything to get kicked out of church, or get me to quit going. The church family (sometimes reluctantly) chose to love him in spite of his many antics and disrespectful attitudes. The pastor wouldn't let them give up on him, or us as a family. That son is a missionary today—teaching others about God's love and ability to restore broken lives and families.

> Another son became rebellious and acted out his anger after his dad left. Men from our church invested in him, took him to ball games and lunches, and mentored him. Life wasn't easy for him—but he found peace in his life when he let go of his anger.

> My youngest son built a wall around his emotions, rejecting any affection. He learned to trust and love again through church friends who brought laughter back into his life and leaders who followed through on promised activities. Our church family restored his faith in God and mankind through patience, honesty, and investment. Today he's a pastor—he's encouraged hundreds of teens and adults going through their own difficult trials.

> My youngest daughter was only two-years-old when her dad left, and she would ask me every night for weeks "When is daddy coming home?" Over time, she learned about her heavenly father—that God is the father to the fatherless! Our church taught her she had value, and she gained self-worth and confidence. As an adult—she served overseas as a missionary to special needs orphans, teaching rejected and abandoned children about *their* Father in heaven who knows them and loves them. She's currently a social worker and foster care liaison.

We were a mess and not an easy family to love or care for in those early days. But a church that lives out God's Word and loves like God can change your life. There will always be those people who say unkind things, but don't let them chase you away from God or the blessings he has waiting for you! There were some of those in my church as well. I often think, "What if I'd left over their words or actions"? Where would my family be today? How would their legacy have changed?

The right church family can make a huge difference in restoring joy and wholeness to your family.

Opportunity

If you've never asked Jesus to be part of your life or your family (or it's time to come back to Him), you can do it right now. A simple prayer is all you need to begin your faith journey. You can pray whatever words are in your heart, but here is a prayer if you need help getting started.

Lord, I admit I need you in my life. I believe God, that you sent your son Jesus to die on the cross to pay the price for my sins. I ask for your forgiveness for my past words, thoughts and actions, and I invite you into my life. I choose to follow you beginning today!

Notes

What first step do you want to take to incorporate faith into your family?

In what ways can you strengthen your family's current faith walk?

Co-Parenting

Chapter 11

Co-Parenting

Because co-parenting from a divorce was never in God's plan, there are no Scriptures that specifically speak to this issue. However, there are many Scriptures on how we should seek peace whenever possible and speak with words of wisdom.

I know there are homes where abuse has taken place and children shouldn't be in the care of or be allowed unsupervised visitations. However, whenever possible, co-parenting with love and civility, not with malice or squabbling—results with healthier, happier children.

I'm approaching this chapter a bit differently than the others as I dissect James chapter 3 to help you see the importance of our behavior when faced with a difficult or even impossible person.

The entire book of James is a good resource on improving our actions, words, endurance, and outlooks, but chapter 3 focuses on taming our tongue. I will also list several suggestions for practical co-parenting helps after we look at James 3:3-18. I want you to read this entire passage because it describes our often-fickle behaviors.

James 3:3-18

When we put bits into the mouths of horses to make them

obey us, we can turn the whole animal. Or take ships as an example. Although they are so large and are driven by strong winds, they are steered by a very small rudder wherever the pilot wants to go. Likewise, the tongue is a small part of the body, but it makes great boasts. Consider what a great forest is set on fire by a small spark. The tongue also is a fire, a world of evil among the parts of the body. It corrupts the whole body, sets the whole course of one's life on fire, and is itself set on fire by hell. All kinds of animals, birds, reptiles and sea creatures are being tamed and have been tamed by mankind, but no human being can tame the tongue. It is a restless evil, full of deadly poison.

With the tongue we praise our Lord and Father, and with it we curse human beings, who have been made in God's likeness. <u>Out of the same mouth come praise and cursing.</u> My brothers and sisters, this should not be. <u>Can both fresh water and salt water flow from the same spring?</u> My brothers and sisters, <u>can a fig tree bear olives, or a grapevine bear figs?</u>

Neither can a salt spring produce fresh water. Who is wise and understanding among you? Let them show it by their good life, by deeds done in the humility that comes from wisdom. But if you harbor bitter envy and selfish ambition in your hearts, do not boast about it or deny the truth. Such "wisdom" does not come down from heaven but is earthly, unspiritual, demonic. For where you have envy and selfish ambition, there you find disorder and every evil practice.

But the wisdom that comes from heaven is first of all pure; then peace-loving, considerate, submissive, full of mercy and good fruit, impartial and sincere. <u>Peacemakers who sow in peace reap a harvest of righteousness.</u>

If you have an ex-partner who will work with you, think of the following examples as instructions, or helps, toward a unified front in raising happy, healthy children. However, I fully understand you may be working with an ex-partner who has no desire to cooperate with you in any way. In those cases, do *your* part as best you can, setting an example for your children, even if your ex chooses not to. I'm not going to say these steps are easy, but I will say you and your children will benefit if you can train yourself in these responses.

"Out of the Same Mouth, We Praise and Curse."

Do you praise or curse your ex to or around your children? When someone pushes you to your emotional edge, or causes physical, emotional, or financial harm, it's hard to keep hate out of your thoughts or vocabulary. But for the sake of your children, you must try. Is this hard? Of course! Is it necessary? Yes! Does it mean you don't take action to protect yourself or your children? Never. But it does mean you should <u>wait until your emotions are under control</u> before reacting or speaking. Walk away, take a breath, consider the outcome before speaking or reacting.

"Can Both Fresh water and Salt Water Flow From the Same Spring?"

The answer is no. Yet there are those places freshwater and saltwater come together in an estuary. Estuaries provide a nesting and nurturing atmosphere to develop new life. <u>Two contrary forces coming together for the good of the life between them.</u> I never knew what an estuary was until I moved to California. Upper Newport Bay had a beautiful park where I could look down on the estuary full of nesting birds, fish, and wildlife. It was such a peaceful, protected, and beautiful place. Even as separated parents I hope you can <u>find an estuary</u> in your differences.

"Can a Fig Tree Bear Olives, or a Grapevine Bear Figs?"

The answer again is no. However, today we know that if you cross pollinate, take the best of two variables (say plums and apricots) you can get the best of both (pluots). You may have a different DNA than your ex, but DNA from both of you is in your children. Avoid sharing (cross-pollinating) each other's flaws, but instead share, emphasize, and utilize each other's strengths to produce the <u>best of both of you</u> in your children.

"Peacemakers Who Sow in Peace — Reap a Harvest of Righteousness."

What is the end result you desire for your home and your child? Peace and words of life, or strife and cruel words? When you strive to guard your tongue, it will result in a life with <u>less regrets and more peace.</u> This is a difficult task when working with a difficult person but do *your* best to achieve this goal so you and your children will reap the benefits.

It's never easy to parent with someone who is not part of your everyday home life or in agreement on discipline, goals, or morals. Co-parenting is done with either two people putting aside their personal issues for the benefit of their children or done with animosity and constant contention. I pray you choose the former for the sake of your children. No child does well when parents are battling over them, or for them.

Co-parenting is a complicated subject because there are so many diverse co-parenting situations. I believe the subject of co-parenting deserves an entire book, of which there are several. Because there are a number of books available on co-parenting, I will leave this topic to those experts. I did not personally struggle with a lot of those issues. I had my kids 24/7 from the time their dad left. He saw them only a few hours each week. Yet we had enough issues from just those few hours that I have great compassion for those parents who suffer through weekends and vacations filled with stress, strife, exposure, and malice.

To encourage you, I've also seen co-parenting at its best. The child came first, and parents were civil, even friendly with one another. Their shared times were cooperative and balanced. The desire to be a good parent, even when the marriage failed, made for healthy parent-child relationships. This is possible when parents put the children ahead of their own feelings or need to be in control. But again, do your part as best you can, regardless of your ex's choices.

I want to give you a few practical ways to co-parent for the benefit of your children.

Be flexible whenever possible, and do not let your children see you as the one keeping them from their absent parent. However, this does not mean you must compromise the safety or the routine that offers security to your child. It only means be reasonable, not stubborn.

Don't use your children as pawns, spies, or message carriers. They should not be the go-between or be put between you and your ex. Even when it's difficult, face your fears and speak to your ex directly, not through your children.

Allow your children to love the other parent. Let them know it's ok with you that they love or want to spend time with their absent parent. You may inwardly hate it, but your children should not feel they must choose only one parent to love. (They want to love and be loved by both and be loyal to both).

Be sure your children know they are not the cause of a breakup, even though they suffer the consequences. Make emotional issues as easy as possible on your children, not more difficult.

Try not to speak negatively to your children about your ex. It often pushes them closer to the absent parent, causes them to resent you, or makes them question your motives. They need love, not hate and anger, filling their minds and emotions.

If there are abuse issues or concerns, contact a social services agency. You may still need to find a good lawyer to protect your children. If you have no money, start with legal aid services. You can also try a good law firm and ask for pro-bono help. If you never ask, you will never receive.

Know your legal rights and boundaries. There are exes who on every visitation expose their children to drugs, various partners, language, violent movies, sex, etc. They seem to flaunt everything you want to protect your child from. Legally, there often isn't much you can do unless it's physically or emotionally affecting your children. Social services may be able to get supervised visitation at that point, but it's a hard-fought battle.

I suggest you get the best support you can for yourself and for your children. Surround them with the best people you can while they are in your care, so they see the benefits of healthier lifestyles.

I suggest if you have problematic co-parenting issues to seek counseling and research books that specifically tackle this subject. You can Google "co-parenting books," order them or check them out at your local library. Seek out the books that best fit your situation.

Pray hard always, especially when your children are out of your home. Pray for them to see truth for truth and lies for lies. Pray against manipulation and pray for their protection. Pray for them to be the influencers—not the influenced.

Ultimately, you must choose to be the best example and leader you can be every moment you have your children. Help them to see positive people's lifestyles. Surround them with healthy families, good friends, and a strong belief system. You may have to find, develop, and nurture these types of relationships. Choose your friends wisely; if necessary, find a new circle of friends, even if it means moving beyond your shyness or reticence to explore new interests.

Problems will always stem from a divorce or separation when children are involved. They are long-term, difficult, and often heartbreaking. Books can offer you good advice and direction; however, God is the mender of broken hearts, and He daily renews your strength and offers you hope and life. The following promises from Scriptures are given to you and your children. Speak them out-loud over yourself and over your children as you work through your difficult co-parenting situations.

The Lord is close to the brokenhearted and saves those who are crushed in spirit.—Psalm 34:18

Because of the Lord's great love, we are not consumed, for his compassions never fail. They are new every morning; great is your faithfulness.—Lamentations 3:22-23

But those who hope in the Lord will renew their strength. They will soar on wings like eagles; they will run and not grow weary, they will walk and not be faint.—Isaiah 40:31

Conclusion

Mature parents, who put their children first, can succeed at co-parenting. Sadly, selfish behavior on the part of even one parent can make life more difficult, especially for the children. When abuse and selfishness are not involved, children reap the true benefits.

Even with a "bad" ex, your children can become strong healthy adults. Since you can only control your behaviors, live your life well. Be an example of kindness through your words and actions to both your children and your ex. This will cause *you* to become the influencer and stabilizing parent.

The following Scripture is how God views those who intentionally harm children through their personal power struggles. I've used The Message interpretation as it emphasizes the importance of a parent's role in a child's life.

"But if you give them (children) a hard time, bullying or taking advantage of their simple trust, you'll soon wish you hadn't. You'd be better off dropped in the middle of the lake with a millstone around your neck. Doom to the world for giving these God-believing children a hard time! Hard times are inevitable, but you don't have to make it worse. —Matthew 18:6

Biblical Example—Genesis 17:5-16

No longer will you be called Abram; your name will be Abraham, for I have made you a father of many nations. I will make you very fruitful; I will make nations of you, and kings will come from you .— Genesis 17:5-6

God also said to Abraham, "As for Sarai your wife, you are no longer to call her Sarai; her name will be Sarah. I will bless her and will surely give you a son by her. I will bless her so that she will be the mother of nations; kings of peoples will come from her.".— Genesis 17:15-16

After years of waiting for this promised child, Sarah tires of waiting and loses sight of the promise. She finally tells Abraham to take her maid servant and have a child by her.[61] This child is Ishmael. Later Sarah conceives and gives birth to Isaac (the son God promised).[62]

Jealousy and strife occur between Hagar (Ishmael's mother) and Sarah. Eventually Sarah asks Abraham to send Hagar and Ishmael away.[63] Abraham agrees, and his relationship with Hagar and Ishmael is forever broken. The contention caused by a divided family resulted in a fostered hatred that divided a nation and has caused thousands of years of wars. Ishmael is recognized by Muslims as the ancestor of several prominent Arab tribes and the forefather of Muhammad. Isaac is the father of Jacob, the father of the twelve sons who make up the twelve tribes of Israel (the Jewish Nation). The fighting in the middle east today began with a broken family who sowed seeds of division, jealousy, hatred, and strife thousands of years ago.

Personal Example

Rob and Linda were both divorced with two children when they met over 20 years ago. However, all four parents involved found a middle ground with their exes that would always benefit their children. This family showed respect to one another (even in

---

61 —Genesis 16:1-5
62 —Genesis 21:1-3
63 —Genesis 21:8-13

their differences). The children shared holidays, special events, and vacations with their blended families surrounded by love and peace. I'll always remember the toast given at the wedding of one of the daughters. Rob thanked his ex-wife for doing such a wonderful job raising their children. If only all divorces could end with couples thinking more of their children's needs than their own personal grudges or bad memories.

These parents *spoke words* of mutual respect regarding their exes. They found their *estuary*, *pollinated* their children with the best of their DNA, and *sought peace* for the sake of their children. Today, all four of their children have wonderful families themselves, because they learned how to handle conflict in a Godly, kind, and healthy way.

Notes

Is there something _you_ can do this week to co-parent in a more healthy and helpful way for the sake of your children?

Letting Go

Chapter 12

Letting Go

Like arrows in the hands of a warrior are children born in one's youth.—Psalm 127:4

If arrows stay in a quiver (protected case), they never accomplish what they were created for. You must let them go so they can soar to fulfill their purpose.

What does "letting go" even mean to a mom? It means you change with your child and help them pass through each stage prepared for their next life stage. It means staying aware and engaged, ready to move ahead when they're ready—without clinging to their past stage of life.

Letting go of one thing also means embracing the new. Change is not all bad; your relationship can deepen with each transitional stage as well. Stay positive about their changes and continue to grow and change with your child.

It can be hard to accept how quickly your children are growing up. They are often ready for their next stage of life before you are. However, you must do your best to help your children transition from each stage of life, by recognizing when the change begins to occur, and be willing to *let go* of the old to make room for the new. It's ok to hold on to your fond memories but allow your child to move beyond them. Children, especially teens, do not want to continuously hear about their former stage. Instead, they need wisdom for their current stage and the issues they are facing.

Today's children have lost years of innocence because of our information age, forcing them to grow up faster than past generations. This needs to be met with parents who are prepared to grow with their children. Learn new technology, vocabularies, and stay up on current events.

Here are a few examples of things to *let go*:

The "mommy" voice. "Sweetie," "baby," (cute nicknames they have outgrown), and the baby talk voice. Yes, I've heard moms' voices suddenly turn childlike when speaking to their teenager (who is cringing).

Hugs and cuddling. Recognize when your public display of affection (PDA) is becoming embarrassing to them. This may carry over in the home as well as in public. Respect their personal space and allow them to choose their comfort level.

Let go of old house rules and make way for new ones that better fit the age and personality of your changing child. You don't eliminate rules—you just reassess what no longer works and establish new rules, boundaries, and consequences.

Let go of your control as your children grow. When they are little you set the tone of the house, the rules, the schedules, etc. But as they grow and become more independent, your control must lessen. You still have the benefit of age, authority and wisdom to override their emotional desires or choices. But no matter how you look at it, the older your children become, the more flexible you'll need to become. A teen who is controlled will most often rebel in one form or another. Take time for discussions on curfews and house rules, but still have the final say as the parent. Letting go becomes a balancing act of staying aware and engaged, without hovering or attempting to control everything for them.

Let go of making most, if not all, decisions for your child.

As you guide and give input to their choices, allow them the final decision whenever possible. This respect will strengthen your relationship because they'll feel you trust them. They may not always make the best choice, but they will not learn healthy decision-making skills if you continue to make all choices for them. Of course, safety comes first—you're still responsible for their welfare.

They may choose to take a class that is a waste of time in your mind, a job that is not the best for them, or make a bad friend choice. As long as their choice is not life (or future) threatening, allow them to decide. Reign them in when necessary, but they often see for themselves, the folly of their choice.

Learning from small mistakes and bad judgments will strengthen their decision-making skills. They *will* be an adult one day soon and need to know how to weigh options and think about the results of their decisions. Pray they learn from their smaller failures or mistakes so as to avoid larger ones.

If you teach responsibility and consequences when they are young, you are naturally guiding them to make more mature choices as they transition between stages.

If they make a really big mistake, allow your love and words of wisdom and encouragement to override your feelings of anger or disapproval. It's hard, but calm yourself before responding.

Letting go is not the same as not paying attention. Stay engaged with them and watch for any major behavior changes. Choices that have life threatening or long-term consequences are the things you need to stay on top of. Get all the counsel and help you can *before* confronting a situation, and know where you want things to end before a confrontation. (See the Trauma chapter on pages 107-110 for more specific information and signs of major behavioral issues.)

As your children move into their teen years, there is even more letting go that needs to take place.

Let go of your role as their "all important person". Your teen still loves you, but they are also making their way toward adulthood

Their friends will become their biggest influence, so ask more questions about their friends and get to know them. Invite them over. Be the host home so you see who they're hanging out with. Nurture a welcoming atmosphere for their friends. You can still have rules, just let those rules grow with your children. If they don't feel welcome, they will find another home to hang out in, a place you'll have absolutely no insight or control over.

Letting go is about holding the reigns, but not controlling the bit as tightly.

Your children will need freedom, with restraint; independence with wise counsel; and understanding, when you're out of patience. The tighter your control, the more they'll push back or rebel. If they believe you don't trust them, communication and cooperation dissolve.

You cannot *make* a teenager do much of anything outside their will. All you can do is direct, advise, pray hard, and love them through even their biggest challenges or mistakes.

Letting go is all about moving along in life, not getting stuck in one comfortable cycle of it.

Life keeps moving, kids keep growing, and we must, as moms, be willing to let go of one stage as we prepare for the next.

There are more helpful tips on preparing for transitions and letting go of your child through each stage of life in Chapter 13 "Parenting Extras—Teens, Adult-Child, and Married-Child".

Conclusion Always remember you are walking a journey with your children, taking them from infant to adulthood. Letting go of one stage will always be part of preparing for the next, for both you and your children. Be equipped and prepared to let go and transition with them for a smoother journey and a closer relationship.

Biblical Example–Luke 15:11-32

This is the story of the prodigal son, who was selfish, rebellious, stubborn, and wanted his inheritance early so he could leave home. The father knew he could not change his son's mind and finally had to let him go, even knowing the destruction his son was headed for. (The tighter the hold, the more resistant the rebellious will become.).

The son took his inheritance and left home, fully confident he "knew better than his father what was good for him." The prodigal made terrible friend and lifestyle choices, squandered his money, and was deserted by his new found friends when his money ran out. He finds himself starving, longing for food thrown out to the pigs. He finally returns to his father in shame and humility, hoping to be accepted as a servant.

You see, if the father hadn't *let the son go,* the son would have continued to be angry and rebel, possibly dragging his brother or others into his folly. The son had no chance of redemption unless the father let him go. But the father continued to pray, believe, and watch for his son's return.

When he saw his son coming home across the fields, he ran to him, embraced him, and celebrated with him, even to the dismay of his faithful son. You see, the prodigal was redeemed, brought back into his family and loved. But even with redemption, there are consequences to our actions. The prodigal had still lost an inheritance to pass on to his future generations.

This is a picture of how God views us when we rebel or run from Him. He continues to love us, patiently waits for us to return, and welcomes us with open arms. There will be many blessings and celebrations upon returning to Him, but there are still losses or consequences that come as the result of our choices. (Not from God's rejection or as punishment, but from the result our choices).

Personal Example

I taught a workshop once that touched on the topic of moms sleeping with their children. We talked about its pros and cons. One of the cons was when and how do you give them their own bed and room? The separation is traumatic—some kids are afraid to sleep alone. The change often takes a long time and may be filled with a lot of tears. I asked, "At what age do you make the separation? At 2, 3, 6, 8, 12 ....?" After the session, a mom came up and said her seventeen-year-old son was still sleeping in her bed. Yes, seventeen! This mother had let an unhealthy situation develop because she could not let go of the mutual comfort this arrangement had caused. Obviously, this was not a good situation, but when you become dependent upon your children, or make them dependent upon you, it restricts healthy transitional stages.

I know this is an extreme example, but it shows the dangers that can develop when you are unable to help your children transition into their next stage of life at the proper times.

Letting go of your comfort, to benefit your children's future is what parenting is all about.

<u>*Notes*</u>

Can you think of one thing you may need to begin letting go of?

What will be your first step?

Parenting Extras

Parenting —*Extras*

Newborns

Chapter 13

Newborn — Extras

For you created my inmost being; you knit me together in my mother's womb.—Psalm 139:13

God knows everything about your baby and has a plan for that little life.

Your newborn is a new beginning, not an ending to your life's story. This is an opportunity to live differently, better, healthier—if you choose to do so.

Your baby may have been well planned, unexpected, or just poorly timed. Regardless of why you have a newborn, you're now tasked with the responsibility of parenting him or her.

My "unexpected" fifth baby arrived while our business was being repossessed, our home foreclosed, and our health insurance had ended. When she was 10 days old, we were forced to move into an unfinished home in northern Minnesota. (Can you say cold?). There was no running water (we hauled all water in), no drains (we carried all water out), no insulation or furnace (we had a wood stove), and no sewer lines (we had a portable satellite—outhouse). This was the most un-timely baby arrival possible, but God was still in control. She brought joy to our family from the moment she was born.

Two years later, when my husband left me, it was that unexpected two-year-old's smiling face and happy nature that got me through my worst days. She'd stand at my bed in the morning and sing songs and wait for me to smile at her. Never underestimate God's plans, even when they don't seem to make sense at the time!

Your little bundle of joy has probably turned your world upside down. Schedules have changed, priorities have changed, and sleeping patterns have definitely changed!

You may feel quite prepared for this new challenge of parenting, or woefully unprepared and overwhelmed by it. Don't worry, you're normal; every parent feels overwhelmed and afraid one day, and totally in control the next.

I will highlight just a few of the issues that can plague moms of newborns. I hope you'll realize you are not alone in your thoughts, fears, or even your situation—all moms struggle with at least some of these issues.

Stress

Being a mom in today's culture is very stressful. Social media and mom groups can sometimes exacerbate a new mom's stress level and fears. The list of things that you "should" do to be a "good" mom seems endless. Remember, most people publicly share their wins, not their parenting mistakes. Research is healthy, but perfectionism, competition, and fear can quickly turn into obsessions—replacing the joys of motherhood.

A crying baby combined with a tired mom is an exasperating experience. Try taking a few deep breaths and sing a calming song (for yourself). You want to avoid a stress-filled reaction to a stressful moment.

Let me just say this: you *will* make mistakes. You will respond poorly from time to time. You may yell at that beautiful bundle of "joy" who refuses to sleep or stop crying. You will not be perfect every day, at every moment; stress and lack of sleep takes its toll. This does not give you an excuse to react poorly, but neither does it make you a "bad mom." We all have our fail moments. If you feel you're losing control and your reactions or thoughts are becoming dangerous or violent, seek medical or counseling help immediately.

There are so many changes taking place at this pivotal point of your life, but don't forget to relax and enjoy these precious moments as well. Your baby just needs to be fed, changed, protected, cuddled, and loved. This was much easier in past decades, when mothers were rarely in the workforce. Today, hurried life schedules, work responsibilities, and sometimes multiple jobs are part of a new mother's daily experience—especially single moms! Take every opportunity to rest, cat nap, and cuddle with your newborn, and it will help alleviate some of your stress. Even in the midst of weariness, enjoy these few short months of the newborn stage.

Books, blogs, and mom groups are great, but common sense and good friends bring balance to your fears and points of stress.

Support Versus Isolation

Every parent, especially single parents, need a support system. You will get tired, you will need a break, you will need advice, and you will need encouragement. Support may come individually or as a group from family, friends, neighbors, or church community. We need each other to grow, to stay strong, to keep perspective, to stay sharp, and to give healthy examples to our children.

Isolation can be a common reaction for new mothers. However, isolation is usually based on fears. It may be a fear of people (they may hurt you again), baby's health (overly protective), perfectionism (nobody can do things as well as you), or a perception of failure (somebody may see your weaknesses). But isolation is always a detriment to an individual and the health of a family.

When I felt so alone, afraid to trust anyone, not wanting to share any of my fears or needs, isolation began to smother me. It was a difficult choice to re-enter the world of people again, that scary place that had caused such deep pain. The old Simon and Garfunkel song, "I am a Rock," had become my mantra for never being hurt again. But it also perfectly describes the loneliness and hardness that follows when you isolate from the world. Here is a portion of that song:

I've built walls—A fortress deep and mighty, that none may penetrate—I have no need of friendship, friendship causes pain—It's laughter and it's loving I disdain—I am a rock, I am an island . . . I am shielded in my armor—Hiding in my room, safe within my womb—I touch no one and no one touches me—I am a rock, I am an island. And a rock feels no pain—And an island never cries.

A rock and an island also experience no joy! If you've isolated or insulated yourself because of past failures, fears, or pain, it's time to slowly pull down your walls. Learn to trust again, become a friend to others, and find your needed support in times of stress.

Depression and Guilt

Guilt is a common and constant companion to most moms, and also her worst enemy. Don't let it have a controlling voice in your parenting life.

Guilt drives poor decisions, low self-confidence, kills goals, and is unproductive. You don't have to read every parenting resource to be a good parent—just be wise enough to seek advice in your personal areas of weakness. Remember, common sense, gentleness, and a healthy support system are your strongest assets. A supportive church family can also stand in the gap if you don't have relatives who are capable or willing to properly advise or help you. Listen to those people whose lives and habits you admire and would like your family to mimic.

Things you never thought about before the baby arrived can become obsessions. The foods you eat, the hours you keep, the friends you choose—they all affect and influence this little life. Articles and blogs fill your mind with fears, guilt, or a hyper vigilance to control. They can cause depression and feelings that you just don't measure up to those wonder moms you keep seeing or reading about. If you feel overwhelmed by guilt or depression when your baby is healthy and thriving, stop reading posts and blogs.

Hormonal changes, along with new schedules and sleep deprivation, can often bring on temporary depression.

However, even in the midst of all your new baby excitement, some moms suffer from postpartum "baby blues" or depression. As the Mayo Clinic reminds us, this not a character flaw, but simply a complication of giving birth."[64]

Here are the symptoms and differences listed for both postpartum "baby blues" and "depression" from the Mayo Clinic website.

To avoid confusing baby blues and postpartum depression read the symptoms and articles noted in the below footnote from the Mayo Clinic website.

Some of the signs and symptoms of *baby blues*, which could last only a few days to a week or two after your baby is born:

Mood swings

Anxiety

Sadness

Irritability

Feeling overwhelmed

Crying

Reduced concentration

Appetite problems

Trouble sleeping

Postpartum depression signs and symptoms may include:

Depressed mood or severe mood swings

Excessive crying

Difficulty bonding with your baby

Withdrawing from family and friends

Loss of appetite or eating much more than usual

Inability to sleep (insomnia) or sleeping too much

Overwhelming fatigue or loss of energy

---

64 Mayo Clinic, Postpartum and depression-signs, baby blues-signs, postpartum psychosis signs. Website: www.mayoclinic.org

Reduced interest and pleasure in activities you used to enjoy

Intense irritability and anger

Fear that you're not a good mother

Hopelessness

Feelings of worthlessness, shame, guilt or inadequacy

Diminished ability to think clearly, concentrate or make decisions

Restlessness

Severe anxiety and panic attacks

Thoughts of harming yourself or your baby

Recurrent thoughts of death or suicide

If you recognize yourself in either of these checklists, talk to your physician for practical help and to monitor your care. Ignoring these feelings can lead to deeper depression, isolation, guilt, and even suicide.

Please seek help if you suffer with continuous guilt, or the realities of postpartum baby blues or depression. Begin with your doctor, but if that's not possible, call a local depression help line or hot line. Don't suffer alone or in silence.

Difficult Baby

Though you want to do everything right, you may have a newborn who just doesn't seem to cooperate. Some babies cry a lot; others don't. Some sleep through the night immediately, most take about four months, while still others wake regularly for over a year. All your efforts to do everything right will not change the personality of your baby. Accept them for who they are and adapt to their little disposition and personality.

Your baby's health will also make a difference. If your baby seems healthy but continues to cry after feedings and a diaper change, check with your doctor. Newborns can have reflux, colic, and other digestive or bowel ailments that cause distress.

My firstborn had colic. I didn't think to tell my doctor he cried even after feedings because I thought this was normal. It wasn't until I had my second son that I realized my firstborn had suffered needlessly because I didn't realize his relentless crying wasn't normal newborn behavior.

A clinic nurse is often willing to answer questions and recognize if your baby needs to be examined by the doctor. You are your baby's advocate, so when in doubt don't settle for googling a medical website—seek proper help.

Nursing

Every mom cannot, for a variety of reasons, breastfeed their baby. If you must formula feed your child, you're still a good mom—and your child will survive. Many healthy young moms today were bottle fed themselves because of their mother's work schedules or inability to produce enough milk.

Mother's milk is the best. However, if there are allergy issues, difficult work situations, or you are not producing enough to satisfy your child, you may need to supplement with formula. (Do so without fear or guilt that you're damaging your child.) Natural is wonderful, when it works. However, it becomes a problem if your baby isn't getting proper nourishment, is constantly fussy, cries often, needs frequent feedings, or becomes lethargic. When nursing is problematic, it wears *you* out both physically and emotionally. Speak to your doctor or nurse practitioner for advice if feedings are not going well.

Keep in mind, a relaxed mom will have a much better feeding result than a stressed mom, regardless of the method or milk used.

I personally had to bottle-feed four of my five children with formula. By the time I had my fifth child, doctors were much more focused on the mother's diet and the overwhelming advantages of breastfeeding. It was difficult for me, but I worked to breastfeed her. I was always concerned if she was getting enough, and that my diet supplied her needed nutrients (my stress level was high at this time and our food budget was low). A plus side to formula feeding was I always knew exactly how much my babies were drinking and that they were thriving. Thankfully, none of my formula-fed children ever developed allergies or ear infections—the side-effects often associated with formula. It helps to pray and trust God for the things we cannot control.

Breastfeeding is naturally the best choice,[65] but if you must use or supplement with formula, don't let worry consume you. My three formula fed sons are 6'2", athletic, and healthy; my formula fed daughter is also a normal, healthy woman, so don't let fear overtake you if you must use formula.

If you have concerns, always check with your doctor to be sure your child's dietary needs are being met.

Sickness or Disabilities

If your baby is sick or was born with a disability, parenting life and routines become even more difficult. You will definitely need direction from your doctor on how to cope and manage not only your child's life, but yours as well. The constant care required can affect your job, your other children, and your health. Use community resources, social services, and any other local resources available to you. Do not resist or fear asking for help.

Small communities may not have as many resources to help, but do not remain alone. Check your local library, clinic, and churches to find the support you need. Finding people who can give you a break in caregiving, encouragement on the dark days, and hope when you feel hopeless is essential.

I encourage you, along with local resources, seek out a church community that will embrace you and your child as part of their family. They can often be your source of physical and emotional relief.

Spiritual Help

I can't explain how faith works. I've just witnessed it in my life and in the lives of so many others going through unbelievably difficult times and circumstances.

A crying baby can jangle anybody's nerves; but worship music

---

65 Mayo Clinic, articles on "Nursing vs Breast Feeding, Which is Best", "Breast Feeding Tips", and "Breast Feeding Nutrition. Website: www.mayoclinic.org

seems to bring calm to a stressful atmosphere as well as everybody's nerves.

Studying God's word through Bible studies or small groups opens your eyes to possibilities and hope, instead of living in weariness or defeat.

Praying brings a sense of release and peace. When problems overwhelm you and you have no answers, pray! (Many times, my prayers were answered, but even when I didn't get the answer I'd hoped for, God brought me peace.) Prayer pushes us towards a level of trust, which allows us to let go of the "control" button we so firmly hold on to as a mom.

When you don't understand God's timing—trust in His faithfulness.[66] When you don't get an answer to "Why?"—God's unconditional love becomes your comfort.[67] When you feel you can't go on—God's grace carries you through.[68]

I speak at many retreats for single moms which are titled "Dare to Dream". We need vision to dream beyond our current circumstance. No matter what stage of parenting you are in, be challenged to look beyond the moment.

God has given you this newborn to love, protect, and nurture. This is an opportunity to adjust your priorities, grow in your faith, and for some moms, change the direction of your life. Find joy in the little things, whatever stage you are in.

---

66 —Isaiah 40:28-29
67 —Psalm 119:76
68 —2 Corinthians 12:9

Conclusion

My final advice for moms of newborns can be summed up here:

Research—but stay calm

Accept joy—reject fear

Sleep revives—nap often

Know yourself—reject guilt

Perfection isn't reality—it fosters stress

Depression is real—seek medical help

Developmental challenges are hard—don't go it alone

Friendships encourage—isolation destroys

Enjoy your newborn—time passes quickly

Notes

Children

Chapter 13

Children — Extras

Children are a heritage from the Lord, offspring a reward from him.—Psalm 127:3

I feel cherish is the word that comes to me for this section. Cherish your "reward", cherish this stage of their life, cherish your opportunities. We sometimes spend so much time in regret or anguish, and we forget to cherish the precious moments of parenting.

These are some additional parenting thoughts for your K-6 boys and girls that might be helpful to you. Again, glean what is useful in your situation, or use these thoughts to generate your own new ideas or habits. Some of the thoughts below may be useful for the man in your child's life—either their dad, uncle, or male role model.

Your Boys

By about fourth grade, boys begin to seek more independence. As they approach middle school you will notice even more distancing from you. This is a normal transition— don't panic.

Boys want to become men. It's in their nature, and it becomes stronger the older they get. They begin to resist being treated as a "little boy" or being told what to do by their "mommy" anymore. This is where the role of a dad is important, but when he's missing, single moms must step up to the task at hand. Your son may love you deeply and respect you greatly, but he also desires manhood. Your man-boy needs to be treated differently now. You'll need wisdom on healthy ways to release him and allow him to grow up.

Moms with sons

Don't embarrass your sons with hugs, kisses, or clinging to them.

They will hug you when they feel comfortable to do so, even in public. It's time to let this become their choice, not your need. Don't get angry if they resist you. It's a normal part of the boyhood to manhood journey.

Don't rush your son's maturing, but don't hold him back.

Let him grow up at his pace, not yours.

At times, boys are messy, impulsive, unintentionally reckless, and crude.

These traits can seem wrong or unnatural to moms, because our nature is to be thoughtful, well-groomed, and nurturing. However, it's these "rough boy" traits that develop strength, character, and purpose in boys. Their God-given nature is to protect and provide. (This doesn't mean dominate or control.) When this role is taken away from them, they lose their purpose. Then as adults, they see no need to be responsible for their children or respectful to the woman who bears them.

We can teach manners without stripping boys of their masculinity. When masculinity is trained, not stifled, your boys grow into strong responsible men, able to face the challenges of life and who desire to care for and protect their own family.

Spoiling your sons does not benefit them.

By doing everything for your son, you are affecting their self-esteem and future habits. We have more adult men today who expect a woman to do everything for them because they were trained to be pampered or catered to by their mama. Spoiling develops a lack of respect, which carries over to their adult behaviors towards teachers, bosses, and mates.

Pampering your son may also include fighting all his battles. Again, this strips them of their masculine nature. This doesn't mean you don't defend or stand up for your son when necessary, but it's more important to teach him how to stand up for himself. (This is true for your daughters as well.) I'm not saying we have to stay in male/female roles at all times, but God created our different natures to be our strengths— complimenting each other. Neither nature is weak, but together we are made stronger.

A male advisor may help

If there is a man who can have a healthy role in your son's life, it will be very beneficial. He can answer questions your son may not want to ask you (i.e.: sexual questions). It could be a relative, friend, or church leader, but he must be someone you trust with your son's development (an example he could follow).

You may also need a male counselor or advisor from time-to-time yourself, to help you better understand and respond to your son's behaviors. I'm not saying to ignore bad behavior, but some behaviors moms may consider bad or inappropriate, are part of the normal male maturing process.

Summary

Don't try to make your boys act and respond like a girl— they are different. Teach them respect towards adults and gentleness towards girls. Their strength is given to help others, not to dominate or harm.

Encourage your sons' maturing process instead of holding them back because of your emotional needs or fears. They will love and respect you for this fearless act of love.

NOTE: Don't fear losing your sons. My grown boys are very close with me, give me hugs all the time, and are very protective of me.

Boys "released" become men who respect and love the mom who taught them to be strong, kind, independent and fulfilled.

Dads with sons

If there is dad or male role model for your son, here are a few words of advice:

Don't expect your son to be you.

Remove pressure to be like you.

Help him discover who he is by exploring different venues or interests.

Let your son enjoy his childhood. Dads can tend to rush the maturing process of their sons—for companionship or play-mate reasons.

Encourage your son's strengths and interests, even if they are not yours.

You are not their buddy; you are their dad (or male role model). They need your guidance, and boundaries that guide them toward healthy life choices.

Set an example of honesty and integrity through your job, with your friends, and through your everyday life.

Protect them. Do not expose them to sexual or violent themed movies, books, or events.

Be wise about the friends you bring into their sphere, the language used, and the lifestyles lived out.

Show respect to women, in both your speech and actions, so they will follow suit.

Boys want to imitate their dad (men), so set an example that will lead him toward a successful and fulfilled relationship and life.

Your Girls

Girls are often insecure about their looks or abilities. They need praise, encouragement and tenderness. This builds their self-esteem, which enables them to make wiser decisions about their life and relationship choices.

Dad's play an important role in a daughter's life, and when dad is missing it can affect her need for male attention and affection. However, a mature mother can build more confidence in her daughter than anyone else by making wise word choices, wise personal choices, and wise friend choices.

If your daughter also knows how God sees her, loves her, and accepts her, she will be less prone to seek love in inappropriate or harmful ways.

Moms with daughters

Set realistic goals:

Your daughter is not you. She has her own personality and goals. Encourage her strengths, even if they're not yours.

Emphasize self-esteem by the boundaries you set regarding appearance, friendships, and value (these will all affect her future dating choices and expecations.)

Looks and appearance:

Bring balance to her world of beauty and its pressure brought on by books (princesses), movies, and even toy ads.

Emphasize the importance of kindness, character, awareness of others, and her giftings more than her looks.

Avoid dressing or acting like your daughter's sister, rather than her mother. Let your daughter see her mom as a vibrant confident woman, not a woman fearful of aging or losing her looks. Remove pressure from your daughter to always look beautiful by not being overly focused on *your* own beauty. Look beautiful mom, just don't over emphasize beauty over character in the eyes of your daughter.

(If you are so focused on staying young yourself, it can lead to clouded judgments on boundaries, wardrobe choices, and disciplines which can adversely affect your daughter.)

We all know the dangerous side affects of a poor body image, so be careful how you emphasize the beauty, talent or fashion styles of other young girls around your daughter.

Hygiene, health, and looks can be highlighted without obsessing over weight and beauty.

Your words are important.

Watch the words you use to describe your daughter, both to her and to others. We can be flippant at times, but words hurt and can greatly affect self-esteem.

Your daughter may be exceptionally beautiful, but that shouldn't be what you brag about. Be wise in what you emphasize. Her value doesn't rest in her looks.

Your daughter may not be a beauty queen, but she needs to feel and believe she is beautiful. Be careful how you describe her to others—she hears you.

Mom's friends matter.

If you're dating, listen to your daughter's feelings towards that man (no matter her age). Is she comfortable around him? Why or why not? Her feelings must come before your emotional or physical needs.

Most runaway girls run because of abuse from a stepdad or their mother's boyfriend. Don't turn a blind eye, or a deaf ear, to her feelings. Be an aware and wise mom.

Your daughter or son may not be ready to accept a man into the family at this time. Waiting to date until your children are out of the home may be a sacrifice you'll have to make. Having to choose between your child and a man you have fallen in love with is always a lose-lose situation.

Patience is needed.

Girls often become mouthy, sassy, and resistant from about 4th grade until at least 10th grade. They are around 'mean girls' at school every day, and it can rub off. It often becomes a method of survival in their world. Avoid letting her "snarky" words affect your reactions. Be patient, always try to teach, rather than react, with your words and corrections.

Girls want and need to be accepted by their peers above everything else. Again, when they feel good about who they are, and who they are in God's eyes, the pressure from others will be less influential.

Dads with daughters

Here are a few tips that will help you navigate your daughter's needs.

Hair matters a lot to girls:

Keep in mind, Caucasian, Asian, African, and biracial hair all require different treatment and care to remain healthy. Check with a salon that specializes in her hair texture for the best moisturizers, styles, and health care.

Hairbrushes matter! Learn which hairbrush is right for the texture of your daughter's hair. Some brushes are very painful. If she has a sensitive scalp, she'll cry (if young, she may even scream) when you brush her hair. This is not her being dramatic—it's a sensitive scalp that is very painful when being brushed or combed. If she's still young, give her a toy to distract her or promise a treat if she can be strong and not scream. Again, the right style of brush and proper moisturizers and detanglers make a huge difference.

Purchase barrettes and hair ties that do not damage or pull hair. Rubber bands pull and break hair (split ends, broken strands); some barrettes snag and pull tiny hairs.

If your daughter has long hair, a ponytail or braid is a simple way to manage it. Pre-teens and teens like special braids. Many of these styles she cannot do herself, even as a teen. You will gain big points with your daughter if you learn to braid. YouTube has many options to help you learn braiding styles. Let her look and choose the ones she likes.

Shampoos also matter. Fine hair, curly hair, or thick hair all require different shampoos. Find the right shampoo and conditioner for her hair texture. Any salon or knowledgeable salesclerk can help you choose the best products.

Try everything before cutting her hair for your convenience.

Clothing matters.

Current styles matter to girls of all ages. Look at catalogs from kids or teen clothing stores to stay current.

If she's responsible, allow her to purchase her own clothes. If she chooses inappropriate clothes, return them, and help guide her to make better choices.

To save money, especially in childhood ages, shop local community Facebook pages for clothes. Many moms sell new, or next to new, name brand clothes online rather than in garage sales. They will describe brands, sizes, and condition of clothes. This is not always an option when they become teenagers, but high quality, name brand, seasonal wear can often be found this way or at consignment stores.

Colors matter.

Skin tone often dictates the colors that look best. Little girls just like to wear their favorite colors. However, if you are buying clothes for your child or tween, keep this in mind. Again, salesclerks are happy to consult with you or your child on this subject.

By helping your middle-schooler begin to see which colors look best on her, she'll begin to select clothes she'll enjoy and wear well. By the time your daughter reaches high school, she's probably choosing her own clothes and you'll lose most of your input capabilities.

Textures/tactile issues matter.

If your daughter has sensitive skin, wool, mohair, and other rough textures will itch and drive her crazy. Listen to her complaints. They are real, and they will be an irritant and distraction throughout her day.

Tags on the back of the neck or waistline can also irritate. Cutting a label out doesn't always get rid of the rough edges. Purchase a seam ripper. (Be careful to rip only the tag and not tear the fabric, or try putting hemming tape over a label).

Emotions and mood swings.

Her menstrual cycle can begin as early as age ten. Prepare them! They may not want to hear about or discuss this topic with their dad. Schools educate, but parents offer wisdom and security. If this is an uncomfortable topic for her to discuss with you, an aunt or other family member is a good option.

Expect mood swings and even diet changes. Various cravings can be common during her period.

For Both

Keep communication open, without being forceful. Natural conversations should become a norm, not the exception. This can occur around mealtimes, bedtimes, or one-on-one outings.

Conclusion

Single parents face so many issues alone. But your journey will be easier when you keep God close and find good friends to help you through each stage of your child's development.

Notes

Teens

Chapter 13

Teen — Extras

Too much talk leads to sin. Be sensible and keep your mouth shut.—Proverbs 10:19 (NLT)

This Scripture is a reminder that all the talking in the world will not *make* a teenager do much of anything outside their will to do. Too much talking only leads to more anger. All you can do is direct, advise, pray hard, and love them through even their biggest challenges or mistakes.

Maybe your teen has become sassier or more resistant towards you. This is another signal of their emotional transition towards independence and adulthood. This is normal, but it will try your patience. Just avoid getting into a snarky word war with them.

Below are a few suggestions for preparing your teen for adult responsibilities. As always, just glean and be creative for your own family's needs.

Driving

Driving is a privilege not a right. They must understand it comes with responsibilities. Their lives and the lives of others are at stake. Remember, insurance and liability claims rest upon you until they become legal adults (or when cars are out of your name and off your insurance).

Decide ahead of time if you or your teen will be paying for the insurance (in part or in full). Teaching your teen the financial responsibilities of driving is also training for independence.

Poor grades will increase insurance rates. If you are paying for the insurance, let them pay the difference if their grades drop. If they are paying, they will quickly learn the importance of good grades. They will once again learn there are consequences to their choices.

Insurance tip: When you transfer a car and insurance into their name (so you are no longer liable), add a life insurance policy to the car insurance policy. At their age, this is a minimal amount and will actually decrease their overall insurance payment (because it becomes a "multiple policy"). Many insurance agencies don't tell you this, but it can be a great cost saver.

Grades

It's hard if your "A" student becomes a mediocre or failing student. You can scream, yell, and ground all you want, but they are going to make choices about how they study at this point. Try the suggestions below and remind them they're limiting their job and college options if they get poor grades. There is no way you can make them do better than they choose to at this age. Now, take a deep breath and relax. Even with poor grades they'll be able to get a college education; it just may not be at their preferred college.

Grounding from activities can be effective for grades lower than C's if they have the ability to get higher grades. That's just laziness and we can't give up trying to motivate them to improve.

If they are just being rebellious or stubborn, passing grades are all you can push for. Usually, even the rebellious teen wants to graduate from high school, and most want to go on to college—they do grow up.

There may be an adult person of influence in their life who can convince them to improve their studies (someone other than their parent).

They have to want to get better grades before they'll put the effort into it. The earlier your child learns consequences for their actions, the easier they'll navigate through academic expectations.

Help them recognize what their giftings are, so they can begin aiming towards a future goal or career they will enjoy. They may change direction along the way and that's ok. They just need to start aiming. Teens with goals do well in school. Those without goals are not motivated to do well, and often become wayward, depressed or fall into drug usage.

Love your teen, even when their grades are unlovable.

Remember, a sudden change in grade or achievements may be a sign of drug or alcohol abuse. (See the "Trauma" chapter on pages 107-110 for signs and help.).

It's hard to see your teen making bad choices, but again, you cannot force them to study or do well. Just keep guiding them in the right direction by encouraging their strengths throughout their childhood.

Curfews and Monitoring

Enforce your curfew times, or they become worthless. One warning rules still apply. (See the "Consistency" chapter on pages 26-28.)

Know where they are, who they are with, what they are doing.

Surprise them by coming home early, see what they are up to when they don't expect you to be there.

Pop into their room even when friends are over (put clothes away, meet their friends, etc.). There is a difference between privacy and secrecy; isolation is not a good sign.

Keep their phones (and laptops) in your room at night. Teens are often texting throughout the night and not getting the sleep they need. Don't let them say it's their alarm clock—buy a clock.

Keep their computer/laptop in an open area whenever possible.

Since they study on their laptop, probably in their bedroom, and the internet is also on their phone, it's harder to monitor but not impossible. There are several tracking and accountability programs available for parents to monitor usage and sites visited by their teen. Check with the phone company, research online, or ask your local youth pastor for advice. Because safety software changes and upgrades often, it's better to ask someone who stays current than for me to try to list any here.

This is not an invasion of privacy; it's responsible parenting to protect your teen from harmful influences. It's no different than knowing who your teen is hanging out with, where they are going, or what influencers are in their life—because that's the description of internet connections today.

Limit the amount of time they are on their computer, especially late-night hours.

Friends

Friends become the single most influential persons in the life of a teenager. Peer pressure can cause even the best teen to make harmful choices. Though you can't choose their friends, try to surround your teen with good influencers. Get them involved in groups and activities that focus on others, rather than self. Broaden their friend base if necessary.

A church youth group can offer them a place where peer pressure doesn't mean compromising values in order to be accepted. Youth groups aren't perfect. They are filled with teenagers from all walks of life, but they are also a place where they are learning their individual value, purpose, and practical ways to set healthy goals into motion. A short-term mission trip to a third world culture will often make a teen more thankful for what they've taken for granted at home. A youth group can be an outlet for your teen's musical, drama, or artistic talents as well.

Give your teen opportunities to become a giver (not always self-focused). Check your local service agencies to find a place that suits your teen's interest. Whether your teen loves sports or the arts, outgoing or shy, there are places for them to be amongst "givers". Examples are Habitat for Humanity, local libraries, food banks, soup kitchens, or the Red Cross. All of these surround your teen with peers who are concerned about others, not just themselves. They build a comradery of acceptance in serving.

Teach your teen (child) that a bully is the weakest of the weak. A bully must hurt someone who cannot defend themselves in order to feel "large and in charge". Always teach respect for others, regardless of others looks, abilities, or aptitudes. A friend who wants to involve another friend in their bullying (or any illegal acts) cares only about themselves and what they want. They will use whomever they can, to get what they want (including their friends). That's not a friend—it's a "user".

Remind your teen that if participating with friends who are caught doing something harmful (bullying) or illegal (shoplifting), they will be found just as guilty. Standing by or watching will not be an excuse or case for innocence.

Always remind your teen of their value in your eyes and God's eyes. This can help them fend off peer pressure to be someone they are not (or don't want to be) just to be accepted.

Express your concerns about a bad influencer but try not to degrade or belittle their friend. If you forbid them to see said friend, it almost pushes them into their arms, and it's nearly impossible to enforce anyway. Pray hard that they see the truth about that person quickly before they are trapped by them.

Prepare Your Teen for Adulthood

Do they want to continue to college? If so, by 10th grade they need to be taking the classes required for college entrance (science, math, and language requirements). They should also be aware that their grades, extracurricular, and volunteer options will influence their college options, applications, and acceptance. In some states, if they are able to take Advance Placement (AP) classes while in high school, they can earn two years of free college credits by the time they graduate from high school—a *huge* financial savings!

(See the "Adult-Child"—College Students section on page 204-205 for more college preparation suggestions.)

If they do not plan on a college education, are they considering a vocational school? If not, what are their plans after their high school graduation?

Of course, they don't need their adult life charted out, and they can change their mind as to careers, schools, and futures. But they must be thinking about their options early enough to make the best choices. Guide your teen to think about their future, their work goals, or college goals. Remember, students with goals make better life choices.

Has your teen been prepared for the discipline of a work world while in high school? If they have not had any work experience during high school because of extracurricular activities, or for other reasons, this can make their transition to adulthood responsibilities more difficult.

Food, cars, insurance, and a roof over their head will never be free in their future life, so prepare them for what's expected after high school well in advance.

You will not help your teen mature into a responsible adult if you continue to let them live a "teen" lifestyle when they complete high school. They need to know and understand your financial expectations and home responsibilities after they graduate (rent/ room and board, living expenses). Learning financial obligations at a young age causes them to become financially responsible as an adult. Most teens won't be thinking about these basic financial facts or expectations without your guidance.

(See the "Adult-Child"—non-college section on pages 205-207 for more specific guidance in preparing your teen for adulthood.)

Prepare your teen for adult life while they are still in school. Don't take away their fun but help them be prepared to make the best possible choices for their future.

Remember, *God will never leave you or forsake you.*,[69] This includes guiding your child through their teen years. Stay close to God for your peace, wisdom, and hope, especially during times of crisis.

---

69 —Hebrews 13:5

General Teen Reminders

The bedroom you once were able to keep clean, tidy and under control may have morphed into a messy, smelly, rat's nest. The state of their room is a small battle you want to avoid; you'll have much bigger battles to fight. However, I suggest you simply have them clean it once a week, by Friday night, so it can be vacuumed. Let them know they are free to do their weekend activities, but only after their room has been picked up. Not spotless—just dirty clothes in the hamper, food removed, floor cleared.

Set a good temperament example for your teen to follow. Actions mean more than words to a teen so live out your words. Work at developing a calm temperament, establish healthy boundaries, and display wisdom. Respect is earned, not demanded, and mutual respect influences behaviors and choices. Love builds the confidence and security needed to overcome peer pressure. A relationship with God develops compassion for others, and a vision for the future (even in the midst of crisis).

Be the parent, not the friend (until they are adults), if it's influencing your decisions. Friends care about what makes your teen feel good right now; parents keep the future in focus (even in the rough spots) and what's best for the long run.

Your friends matter! I can't over emphasize how your friends influence your children. Be wise in whom you surround yourself with, especially during their teen years. Do your friends cause you to be a better mom to your teen? Are your children learning good habits from them—what is their influence? Do your children feel safe around your friends? Do they inspire your children and build their confidence?

Mistakes will be made. If you've blown it as a parent, ask God and your child for forgiveness, then—let it go. You cannot change the past. But you can now make better choices, become a better example, and open the door for healing and reconciliation with your child (regardless of their age).

Always let your teen know you love them, even when they make mistakes or bad choices.

Take an interest in their interests. Let them know you care about what they care about. Attend activities whenever possible, even if they're boring to you. Help your teen pursue their dreams.

Spend time with your teens. Take them places they'll enjoy, learn about the topics that interest them, and listen to their heart.

These habits all build value, respect, and confidence in your teens and a stronger relationship between you.

Remember to have fun with your teen. You may be surprised how much they enjoy doing things with you when they have input and are not "guilted" into activities.

Conclusion

Teen years can be very enjoyable, even in the midst of the angst. Just choose your battles wisely, lighten up when you can, be firm when necessary, be patient when you're exasperated, and be loving as much as possible. Pray hard and never give up!

Remember, you can do everything right as a parent, and your teen can still make poor life choices. However, if you surround them with a safe environment, sound friends, and solid instruction— you've given them every opportunity to make good life choices.

<u>*Notes*</u>

Adult Child

Chapter 13

Adult Child — Extras

When I was a child, I talked like a child, I thought like a child, I reasoned like a child. When I became a man, I put the ways of childhood behind me.—1 Corinthians 13:11

This Scripture puts life into perspective well. There comes a time when childish behaviors, habits, and reasoning must be set aside. This section will look at ways to help your child transition into adulthood, whether they are attending college, working, or not working or contributing after high school.

Once your child graduates from high school, they legally become an adult child moving into their next phase of life—independence and self-sufficiency. As a parent, we know they still need us, but as the adult child, they most often feel they do not. This is why you must be wise and limited with your input or advice in their lives. If you continue to parent as if they were still teens, they often pull away completely from you.

But along with their independence, they are normally still financially dependent upon you, especially if they are furthering their education. So, begin taking steps early to help prepare your teen for adulthood, which will make life easier and liveable for both of you. (See the "Teen Extras" section on "Preparing Your

Teen for Adulthood" on pages 197-198.)

The hard part will be letting them go—joyfully. As single moms, it's hard to let our kids go; we've invested so much of our lives into theirs. When you don't have a life partner, it's easy to make that child your emotional partner. They become the person we share our day with, our story with, our interests with, and when they leave, you can feel abandoned again.

But in order to keep your adult-child close, you must let them go. Holding on too tightly only makes them want to fly further away. I once heard someone say, "Parents don't cut the apron strings—their children do." If we let them go gracefully, the cutting is much easier for both, and the connection remains stronger.

College Students

Allowing your college student to live at home for free may be the only way you can financially help your child through college. However, they should still be working to help out with food (if that's needed) and their personal needs. (Keep in mind, child support will normally end at the age of 18.)

Even if you can afford to pay for their college education, or they have full scholarships, a job is the best way for them to learn about real life living expenses. Their study time is important, but a part-time job will not hurt their studies. It's normally their social time that cuts into study time, much more often than work time.

Your student should be applying for college in the fall of their senior year, getting the Free Application for Federal Student Aid (FAFSA) paperwork done as early as possible so they know what scholarships they can apply for. Visit campuses in the spring of their junior year or the fall of their senior year. This is when many universities host "College Days" with special activities designed for students checking out their college options. By waiting too long or applying too late, your student could lose out on their desired school, miss scholarships, and even miss a year of college. Remember, it's hard to get back into the school routine if they miss a year or want to take a semester or year off.

Prepare your teen for college throughout their high school

career. Guide (not order) them toward the most financially fiscal school that fits their future job goals. Prepare them to live a life independently from you, even when it's hard for you to let them go. That's how you'll keep them close.

Non-College Adult

As their parent, it is your job to prepare them for adult life. Help them think and make choices that will give them a better career. Let them know what you expect of them after high school.

If your teen/adult is not going on to a vocational school, community college, or university, they should be preparing to work fulltime upon graduation. Guide them towards a career that will give opportunities for advancement and a living income. Help them seek jobs that will fit with their talents, personality, and skills. If they enjoy their job, they will flourish in it.

Mechanics, plumbers, and electricians make excellent wages and are in great demand. Some require technical school, but many "trades" jobs have a variety of apprenticeship or training programs. Construction workers also do well, but the work is often seasonal and grueling; they also have physical limitations over the years, unless they become project managers or supervisors. Retail and fast food will only support them if they get into managerial positions. If they begin while in high school, they can often be moving up the ranks toward manager positions soon after graduation. Office jobs can also support them, and if they take a few extra accounting or computer classes, this will raise their income potential. There are also many jobs that will pay to further their employee's education (nursing home staff, warehouse positions, drivers, and several fast food restaurants often have educational helps).

There are many jobs available that don't require a college education, and your teen can pursue those possibilities while still in high school. Cast vision for your teen to consider, listen to guidance counselors, and allow your teen to see their career options and potentials.

Let your teen know you expect them to pay room and board if they live at home after high school. This sounds harsh, but it really prepares them to live on their own, manage their money, and see the realities of living expenses while still in a safe environment. You can choose to use that money towards their expenses or save it. You can surprise them by giving them this money for a first/last month deposit on their own apartment when they are ready to move out.

I'm not saying to throw your kids out the door after they graduate from high school but prepare them for adult living while in high school.

Teens constantly remind you, that they are now an "adult," so you need to remind them that adults have responsibilities, and working is one of them. Again, if *you've prepared them well*, this won't be so difficult for them to understand.

The Non-Contributing Adult Child Living at Home

If you've got a grown "adult child" still living at home, and not contributing towards room or board, then it's time to give them some ultimatums. There is no reason you should be working all day, while they (as an adult) do not work or contribute to the household expenses. Living without responsibilities, or a respect for you, is not benefiting them in the least. They remain dependent, become lazy, and feel they are entitled to what you have, without working for it.

I suggest giving them a time limit to find a job and a place of their own to live, or at a minimum, pay substantially for their room and board. Give them up to six months to be on their own. This will give them time to get on their feet, earn enough money for their first and last month rent, and find a roommate if needed. They will probably need a roommate until job promotions allow them to live on their own, or they get married and have two incomes.

Your "adult-child" needs to understand that it's not your job to support an able-bodied adult indefinitely. You need to understand, by allowing them to remain dependent upon you, their maturation process will become stunted, along with their future.

Choosing a career should be an exciting next step for a prepared young adult. Finding a job that provides for daily needs is a requirement for all adults. These are not cruel or unjust requirements. They are, however, requirements to becoming an adult in more than just age.

Statistics state that "30 is the new 19."[70] Sadly, that means 30-year-olds are at the maturity and independence level of what earlier generations were at 19 years of age. This is caused by parents not equipping their teens to become adults, and a society that makes excuses for immature behavior much longer (entitlement or lack of responsible awareness.)

Parents desire to do what's best for their children. However, faulty parenting happens when guilt, shame, or emotional ties get in the way.

Guilt occurs when you feel you've failed your child in some way. Guilt you cannot meet their every need or want because of financial lack, your work schedule, or where you live. Single moms take on more guilt because you can feel your choices or circumstances are limiting or depriving your kids. You try to overcompensate for these feelings of guilt by going into debt you cannot get out of trying to satisfy unrealistic desires. Some moms are guilt driven to overwork or overschedule to the point of exhaustion trying to 'please' their children.

You will make much better parenting and life decisions when you are not making them out of guilt. *Therefore, there is now no condemnation for those who are in Christ Jesus.*[71]

Shame and failure are sisters. They work together to tear down confidence and wise decision-making skills. They cause a parent to become lax or indifferent, with a "never win" or victim mentality. This is easily passed on to your children. You are freed from shame when you bring your weaknesses to the Lord.

---

70   Market Watch, (2017, July 19). 5 charts that prove that today's 30-year-olds are not adults., https://www.marketwatch.com/story/4-charts-that-prove-that-todays-30-year-olds-are-not-adults-2016-06-30

71   —Romans 8:1

His sacrifice on the cross redeems your failures and gives you strength to face new challenges. The Apostle Paul wrote this next passage when he was plagued with a "thorn in his side." He'd prayed for God to take it away. This "thorn" was humbling because Paul could speak words of healing to others, but not himself. He carried this "failure" with him until God set him free with these words: *Three times I pleaded with the Lord to take it away from me. But he said to me, "My grace is sufficient for you, for my power is made perfect in weakness." Therefore, I will boast all the more gladly about my weaknesses, so that Christ's power may rest on me.*[72] Paul no longer lived in shame or failure but instead overcame his "weakness." He chose to rely on God to get him through his difficulties and feelings of failure.

Emotional ties occur when your life is too entwined with your child's. Parents who fear losing relationship with their children can unintentionally sabotage a successful life for them, or find they've driven their children away. Smothering or being a "helicopter" parent to your teen or adult child is the best way to drive them away (or keep them eternally dependent upon you). Letting go is an integral part of raising healthy children who want to keep a relationship with you. Know when it's time to let go and do it gracefully; make it easy for your children to become adults, not more difficult.

An entitled adult has been taught by society, teachers, and often parents that their (the child's) rights supersede those of everybody else.

The truth is that every individual is important, what benefits the family is important, working together is important, and having goals is important. Trying to make a "child" always feel good is not only impossible but unhealthy for them. A child (adult) becomes self-centered when they are made to believe they are the all-important person in the world. They will probably never find satisfaction in a relationship because they will expect that person to meet all their needs. That is an unrealistic and unhealthy role for any human being.

---

72 —2 Corinthians 12:8-9

Mistakes

None of us are perfect! All parents wish they had done or said some things differently. Even though you can't go back and change the past, you can make better choices for yourself and your adult-child in the future. Make the best of your relationship by forgiving mistakes made by either of you. Accept what you can and cannot change and live in peace. *If it is possible, as far as it depends on you, live at peace with everyone.*[73]

Conclusion

Do as much as you can to help your child transition into the adult world. Prepare them, guide them, love them, and release them. Don't allow guilt or shame keep you from being the parent you desire to be. Let go of your mistakes, let go of their mistakes, and always move forward with hope.

---

73 —Romans 12:18

Notes

Married Child

Chapter 13

Married Child — Extras

Therefore, a man shall leave his father and mother and is united to his wife, and they become one flesh.—Genesis 2:24

This Scripture encapsulates the cycle of life. The next generation is always coming, and you must prepare yourself for it.

You've come a long way in your parenting if you're at this stage. I just have a few simple, basic tips for parenting your married child.

As mentioned earlier, let them also go with grace and ease. They are not yours to keep but to share with the world and eventually their own family. The suggestions I list below are practical suggestions for keeping a close relationship with your married child.

Mates

Accept and love your child's spouse, or risk losing all relationship. No matter the faults you see in their mate, verbalizing them will only drive your child closer to them and further from you.

Since women are most often the relationship builders in a family, your daughter-in-law and daughter may be the one to determine the amount of time you have with your married children. Be wise with words you cannot take back.

A daughter or son-in-law will always know how you feel about them, regardless of what you say. Facial expressions can say it all!

Input

Refrain from giving advice unless you're asked. Most often, if you have a good relationship and don't butt into their affairs, they will not hesitate to ask advice on things they're unsure of. But the best rule of thumb—don't offer unless you're asked. If they're not asking, that usually means they don't want your opinion. On rare occasions, it's okay to give advice when you have experience that will help them. The key word is "rare", share your input once, then let it go.

Don't interfere or participate in their arguments.

Remain neutral, and don't allow yourself to carry their burdens. Pray for them, their issues, and for eyes to be open, but then give it to God.

You are not created to carry the stress of your grown children. They must live with their own choices and lifestyles. If they ask for your help, and you're able to help without enabling a habitual situation, do what you can. Guard your heart and set up boundaries so you don't become their dumping ground for excuses or blame. Shifting their responsibility to you is immature and telling you things you cannot change while refusing advice or help is selfish.

Refrain from telling them what they "should" be doing, or what they're doing wrong. Speak your thoughts, corrections, and ideas in ways that build them up and does not diminish their role as an adult, spouse, or parent.

Visits

Don't overstay your welcome. Whether you are at their home for an event, a chat, or an extended visit, know when it's time to leave.

Some married children like short visits, some longer. Length of stay doesn't determine their measure of love; they all have different stress levels, personalities, and are in various life stages. Be sensitive to their current status and needs.

It's time to leave if you become too comfortable giving your input. It's their home, their rules, their relationship—you're the interloper. If you're a strong personality, you'll have lots of opinions. If you're unable to butt-out, even in your mind, it's time to head home before frustrations flow into words you'll regret.

If you're on an extended visit, remember to give them privacy and space for personal time and discussions. Use wisdom and discernment and know when to leave. This will allow you to become a welcomed visitor rather than a dreaded one.

Grandparent Role

Here comes the hard one. Avoid trying to parent their children—your grandchildren. Just love them. You may have a much better parenting method, at least in your mind, but you had your chance to parent. Accept the role of grandparent gracefully; release the responsibilities of parenting to your grown child.

Always avoid contradicting a parent's decisions, especially in front of the grandchild. You will also become unwelcome if you constantly purchase items you know their parents don't want them to have.

Keeping silent is harder in today's culture. Grandparents don't often have the same position of honor or respect as past generations. Parents today are more educated and believe that trumps elderly wisdom. Philosophies have drastically changed and may be counter to a grandparent's way of thinking. Neither is wrong, they are just different, and you must learn to navigate these differences.

In short, let your married child parent their child in the manner they choose (unless there are issues of abuse).

Your "child" has the responsibility to care for and protect their family. They should, and will, choose their family over you, so tread carefully.

General Help

Each "child" is different. Their needs are different, and they express their love differently. What you need is not always what they need. Their stress may interfere with their communication and responses and have nothing to do with you. The more expressive child who calls often does not necessarily love you more than the distant child—they just express love differently.

Find your own interests so you are not waiting for your "child" to fill *your* needs. You won't be forgotten, but their spouse and children are now their main focus.

You will be honored and loved when you give your married children the respect and space they deserve and need.

Conclusion Here are a few simple things to remember as you parent your adult and married-children.

Express your love—sometimes from a distance

Forgive their choices—consequences will be theirs

Be patient—silence is golden

Keep in contact—even when it seems one-sided

Reconcile your differences—bitterness grows

Be a positive voice—negative words come too easily

Know when to step back (space)—Or when to step up (help)

Embrace text messages—when you long for a call

Visit wisely—accept their boundaries and house routines

Never give up on them, their spouse, their children or your relationship. Keep praying.

Notes

SUMMARY

I hope this book has given you some new insights and helpful ideas as you are raising your children.

These are obviously not all the answers, or even the perfect answers, but *they are a beginning.*

Parent well, forgive yourself, set healthy boundaries, transition with your child, and love them even when they're difficult.

I pray for wisdom and blessings on your personal parenting journey.

ABOUT THE AUTHOR

Lois raised five children as a single mother. Her children were between the ages of 2-11 when her husband left; she was penniless, and on the brink of an emotional breakdown. Fear, grief, and overwhelming responsibilities loomed in front of her. She saw no future, only a lonely and desperate life. Life as she knew it had come to a screeching halt, and yet she had five confused, angry, grieving children looking to her for hope and stability.

Her life changed when she stepped into a church that gave her hope and started her on a journey of healing and wholeness. This church family loved her very unlovable family. They prayed, encouraged, counseled, and became her best friends and family. The church hired Lois, a broken mother, to be their janitor, to financially and emotionally help her out. Five years later, she was hired as their Associate Pastor. God is truly the God of restoration when we put our trust in Him!

Today Lois is a speaker, author, and minister, bringing hope and life to other single moms across the country. She now lives in Florida and continues to write encouraging resources for single moms. She also has developed training materials to better equip churches to reach, restore, and love the single parent families of their communities.

Follow her ministry at www.singlemamas.org or loisbreit.com

Her Bible studies and devotional books are available in English and Spanish for individuals and groups on Amazon.com

Made in United States
North Haven, CT
03 March 2023

33456569R00122